This is a Carlton Book.
Text, design and illustration

Published in 2016 by Carlton Books Limited,
an imprint of the Carlton Publishing Group,
20 Mortimer Street, London, WIT 3JW.

A catalogue record for this book is available from the British Library.

ISBN: 978 1 78312 198 4

Printed and bound in China

Author: Anna Brett
Illustrations: Rebecca Wright
Design: Jacob Da'Costa
Editor: Alexandra Koken
Owner of koob: ....
Favourite page: ....
Page you'd give to a friend: ......
Page that really made you think: ....

Picture credits: Images courtesy of Istockphoto.com p113 & Shutterstock.com p4 (flying fish), p6 (dog), p78 (wood texture).

EXCUSE ME, DID YOU OPEN YOUR KOOB ON THIS PAGE? I BELIEVE YOU'RE NOT THINKING UPSIDE DOWN! FLIP THE KOOB ON ITS HEAD AND START AGAIN. YOU'RE WELCOME.

Stand on your head or do a handstand. Get a friend or parent to take a photo of you. Print it out and stick it in this frame.

CONGRATULATIONS

on completing this koob uʍop ǝpᴉsdn!

THIS IS AN UPSIDE-DOWN BOOK.
THIS IS AN UPSIDE-DOWN BOOK.

BEFORE YOU TURN THE PAGE YOU MUST EITHER:
BEFORE YOU TURN THE PAGE YOU MUST EITHER:

A) STAND ON YOUR HEAD
A) STAND ON YOUR HEAD

B) PUT YOUR GLASSES ON UPSIDE DOWN
B) PUT YOUR GLASSES ON UPSIDE DOWN

C) BE PREPARED TO READ THE BOOK IN A MIRROR
C) BE PREPARED TO READ THE BOOK IN A MIRROR

OR, YOU COULD JUST ROTATE THE BOOK
AND EVERYTHING WILL BECOME CLEAR!

OR, YOU COULD JUST ROTATE THE BOOK
AND EVERYTHING WILL BECOME CLEAR!

upside down | *adverb and adjective* |

With the upper part where the lower part should be; with the top at the bottom and the bottom at the top; the upper and lower parts reversed in position; placed so the end that should be at the top is at the bottom; in or into total disorder and confusion.

DRAW WHAT THE WORLD WOULD LOOK LIKE IF FISH LIVED IN THE SKY AND BIRDS SWAM UNDERWATER.

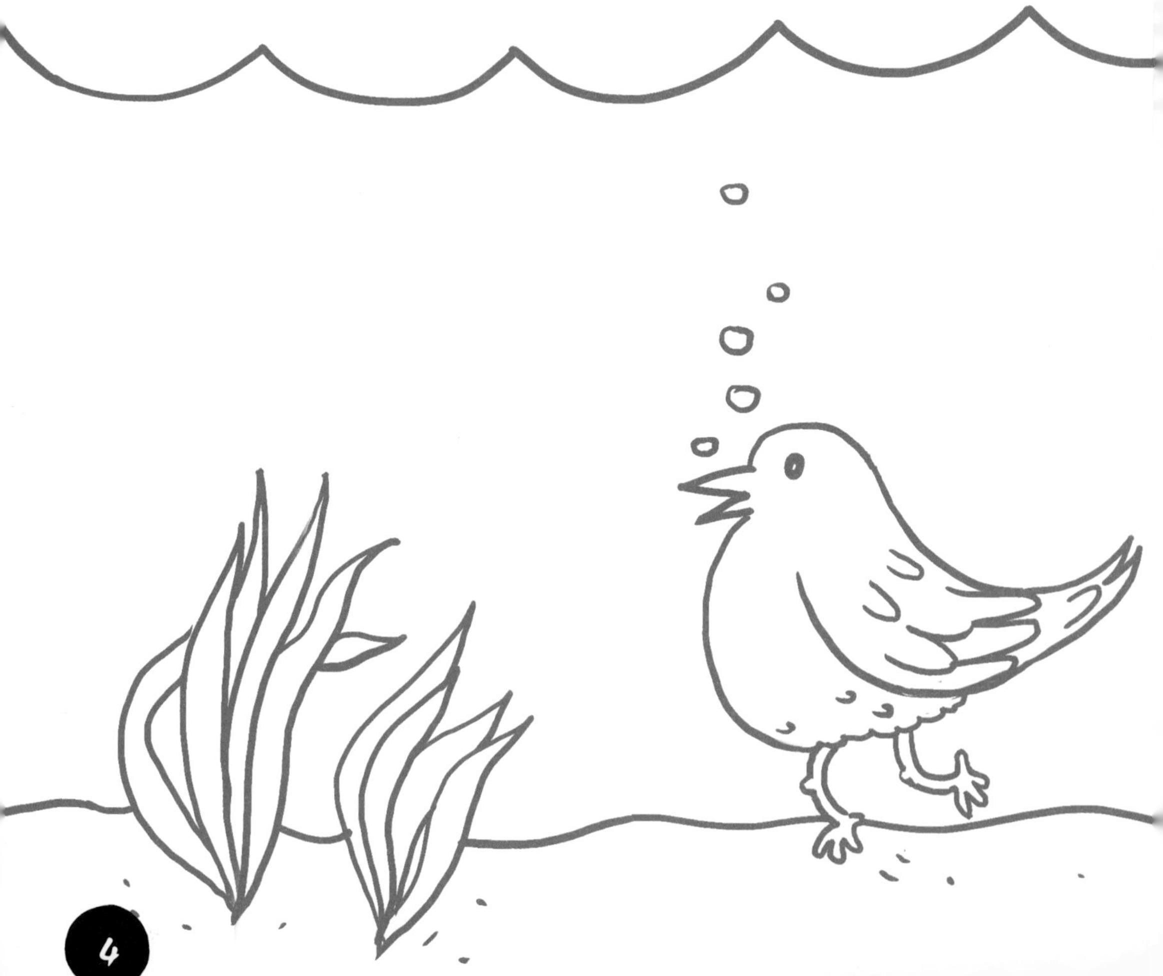

WRITE THIS SENTENCE UPSIDE DOWN THREE TIMES.

The quick brown fox jumps over the lazy dog.

1. **TURN THE PAGE UPSIDE DOWN** AND WRITE THE SENTENCE HERE:

....

2. **STAND ON YOUR HEAD** AND WRITE THE SENTENCE HERE:

....

3. WRITE ALL THE LETTERS IN THE SENTENCE **UPSIDE DOWN**:

....

WHAT WOULD HAPPEN IF YOU ATE A SLICE OF BREAD STOOD ON YOUR HEAD?

WOULD IT POP OUT OF YOUR EARS?

Why not watch your favourite TV show uʍop ǝpᴉsdn! No need to stand on your head... just try this.

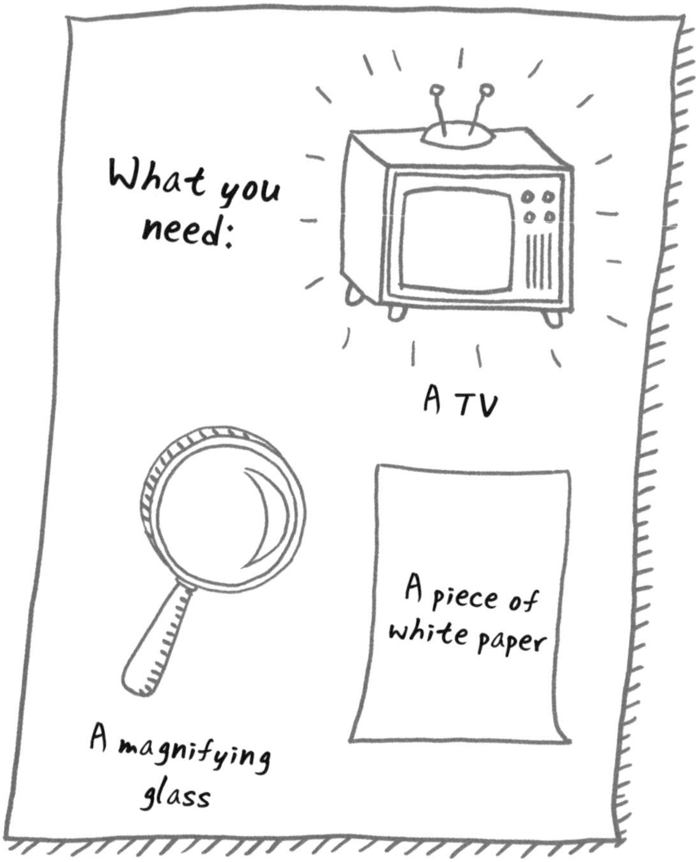

What to do:

1. Turn off the lights and turn on the TV.
2. Hold the magnifying glass in one hand and the paper in the other and stand about 3 m away from the TV.
3. Hold the piece of paper about 15 cm behind the magnifying glass. Both should be at right angles to the floor.
4. Move the paper back and forth until you get a clear image... your show is now playing uʍop ǝpᴉsdn!

LOOK UP! WHAT CAN YOU SEE IN THE CLOUDS?

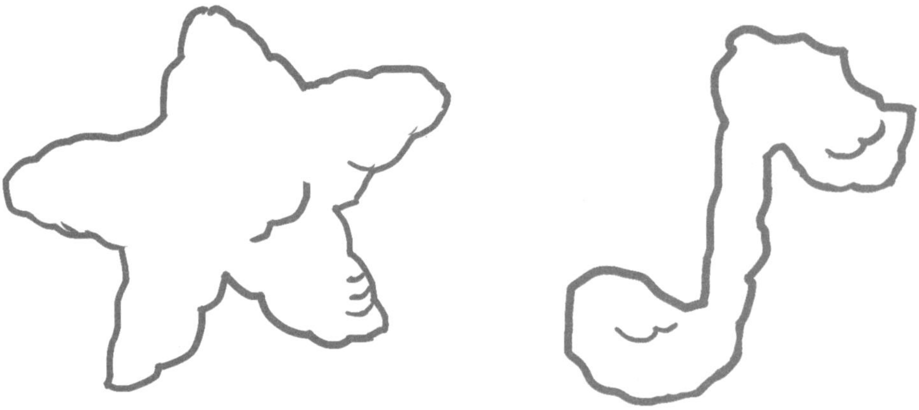

DRAW THE OUTFITS ON THESE GYMNASTS. ARE THEY ON CORRECTLY, OR UPSIDE DOWN?

DON'T FORGET THAT GRAVITY MIGHT PULL THE CLOTHES DOWN!

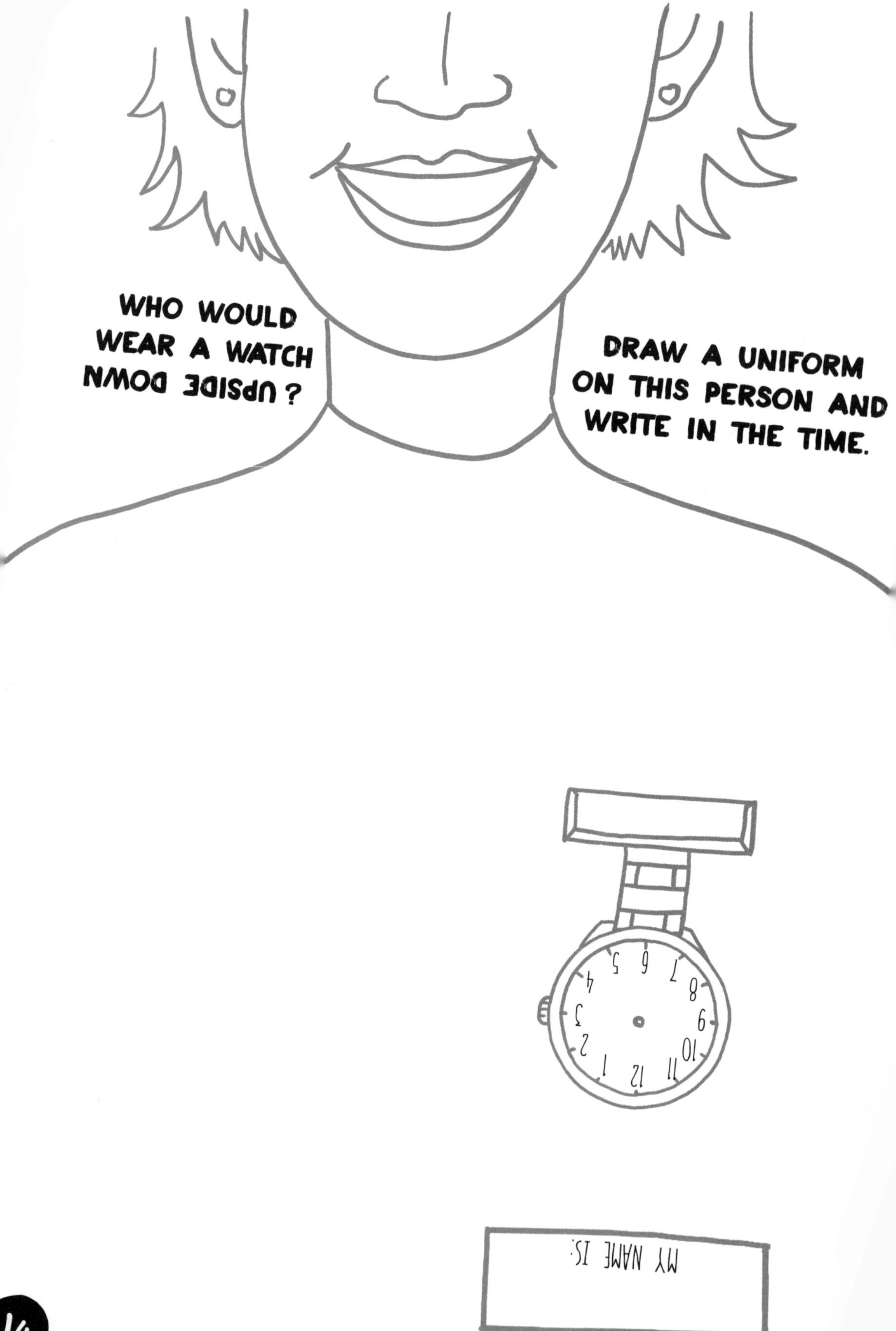

WHO WOULD WEAR A WATCH UPSIDE DOWN?

DRAW A UNIFORM ON THIS PERSON AND WRITE IN THE TIME.

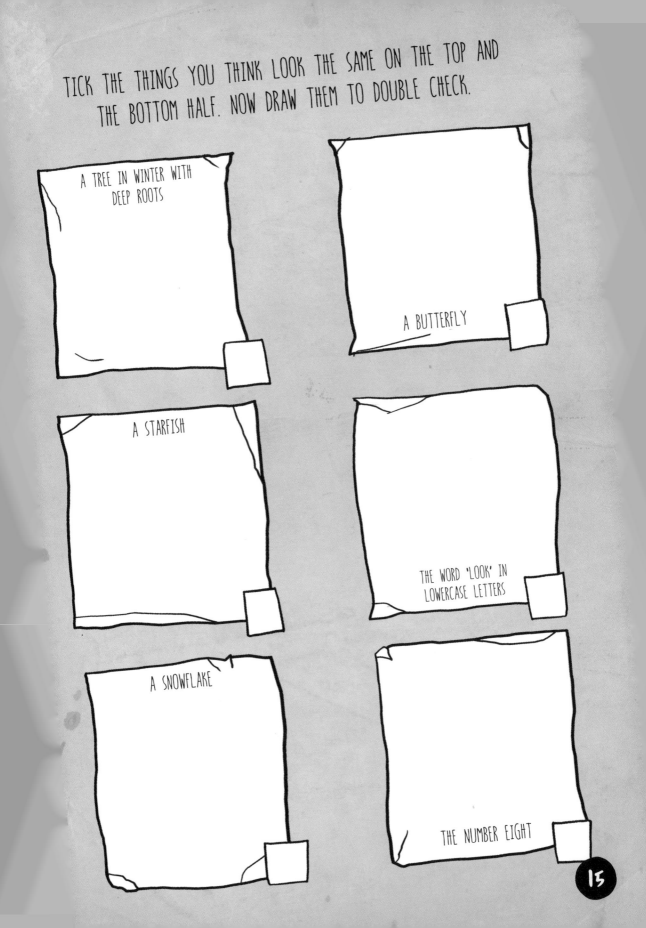

TICK THE THINGS YOU THINK LOOK THE SAME ON THE TOP AND THE BOTTOM HALF. NOW DRAW THEM TO DOUBLE CHECK.

A TREE IN WINTER WITH DEEP ROOTS

A BUTTERFLY

A STARFISH

THE WORD 'LOOK' IN LOWERCASE LETTERS

A SNOWFLAKE

THE NUMBER EIGHT

① Write four dares in uʍop ǝpısdn letters in the triangles marked on the next page. (How about: sing a song backwards, say goodbye when you mean hello...)

② Write eight colours uʍop ǝpısdn on the four outer corners of the big square.

③ Write four numbers in ǝpısdn uʍop letters where marked.

④ Cut out the square along the lines marked with a scissor icon.

⑤ Turn the square around so the lines face away from you and fold like this! The dotted lines will help you...

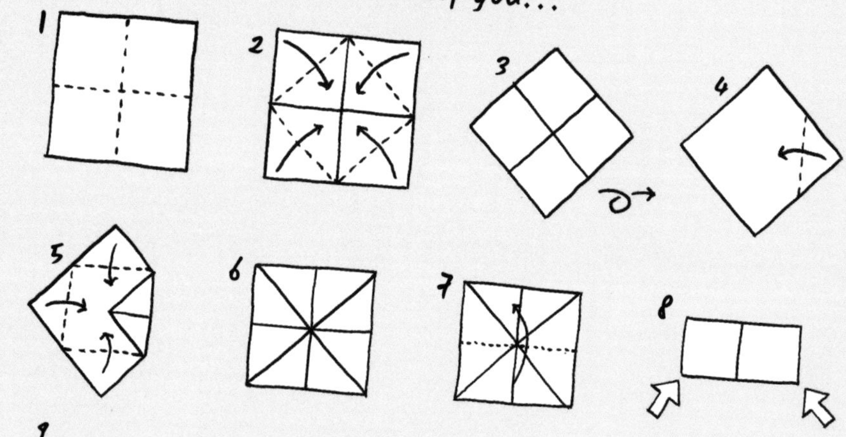

You've made a cootie catcher!
To play, ask a friend to pick a colour, then spell it out. Then ask them to pick a number and count it out. Finally pick a number and open the fold to reveal their ᴧbƨiqɘ qoʍᴎ dare.

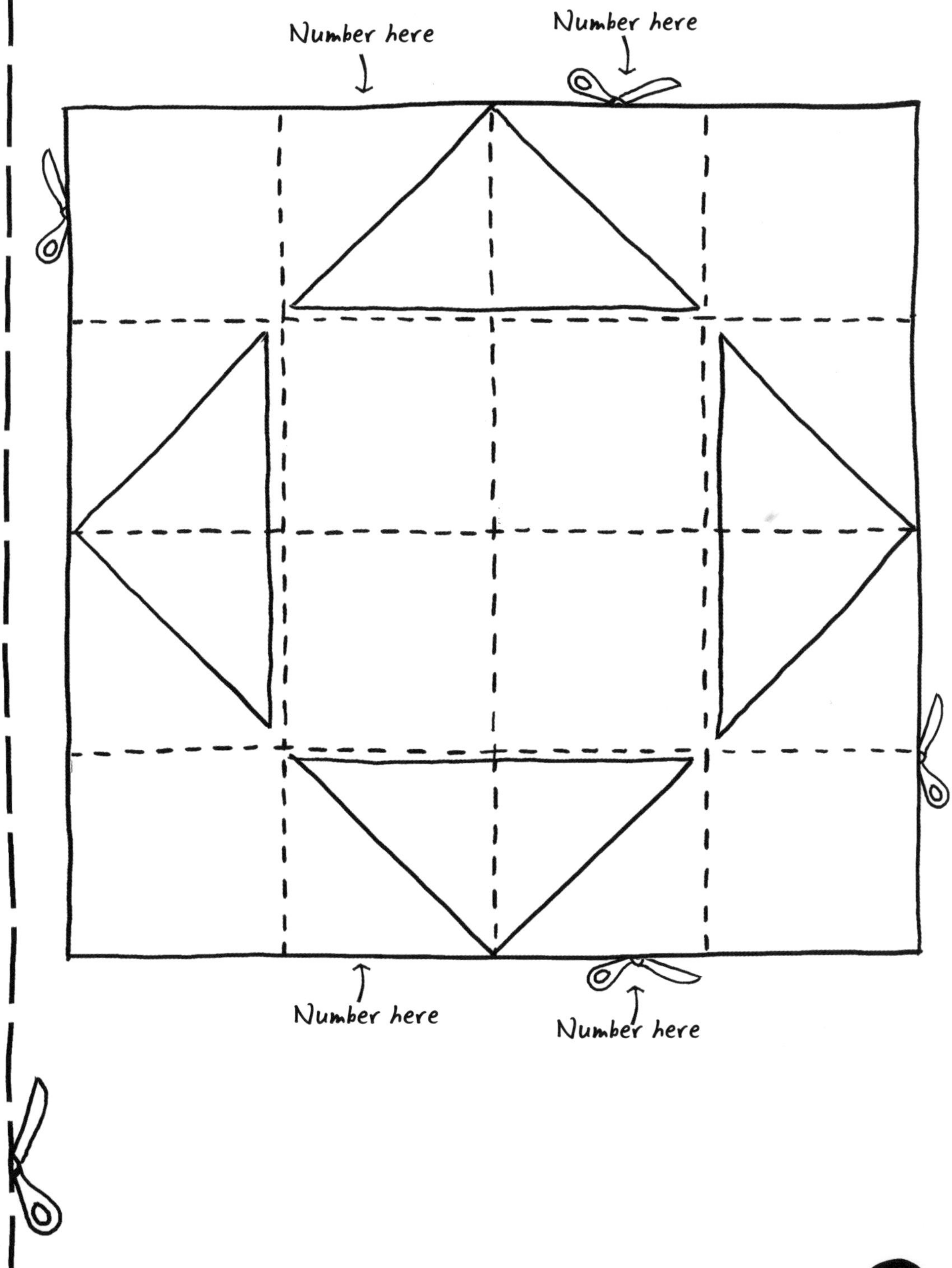
Number here
Number here
Number here
Number here

USE YOUR LEAD PENCIL UPSIDE DOWN.
DOES IT WORK?

STARE AT THIS PAGE FOR 10 SECONDS.
TEAR IT OUT AND STICK IT IN UPSIDE DOWN.
WHAT'S CHANGED?

CAN YOU:

PUT 2 AND 2 TOGETHER TO MAKE A FISH?

PUT 7 AND 7 TOGETHER TO MAKE A TRIANGLE?

PUT 3 AND 3 TOGETHER TO MAKE EIGHT?

ANSWERS: 

How many letters in the alphabet look like other letters when drawn uʍop ǝpısdn?

I guess: ......

Now draw the alphabet to see if you guessed correctly.

Answer: 8

b = g, d = p, m = w, n = u, p = d, g = b, u = n, w = m

UNSCRAMBLE THESE WORDS TO FIND OUT WHAT ACTIVITIES YOU CAN DO UPSIDE DOWN.

1. MWIS KSACOBKTRE

....

2. DERI A LLREOR TSRECOA

....

3. OD A DSAHTDNNA

....

ANSWERS:
1. SWIM BACKSTROKE
2. RIDE A ROLLER COASTER
3. DO A HANDSTAND

LOOK AT THIS INK SPLAT UPSIDE DOWN
AND TURN IT INTO AN ANIMAL.

TURN ALL THE CLOCKS IN YOUR HOUSE UPSIDE DOWN FOR THE DAY AND ASK YOUR FAMILY MEMBERS TO WEAR THEIR WATCHES UPSIDE DOWN.

SEE IF ANYONE IS LATE FOR SCHOOL OR WORK!

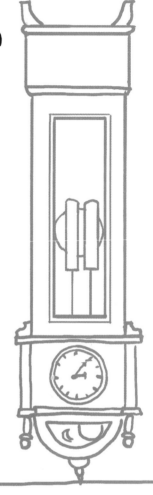

1. TIME YOURSELF SAYING THE ALPHABET BACKWARDS.

TIME...........................

2. TIME YOURSELF SAYING NUMBERS 1–26 BACKWARDS.

TIME...........................

THIS IS SURE TO TURN YOUR BRAIN UPSIDE DOWN - INFLATE AND DEFLATE A BALLOON WITHOUT BLOWING AIR INTO IT!

What you need:

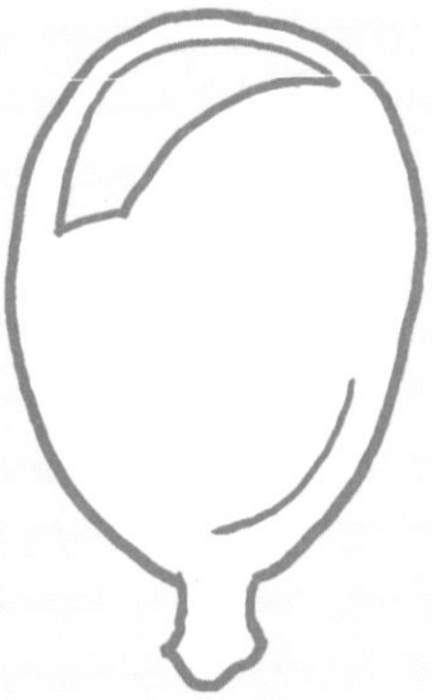

A balloon

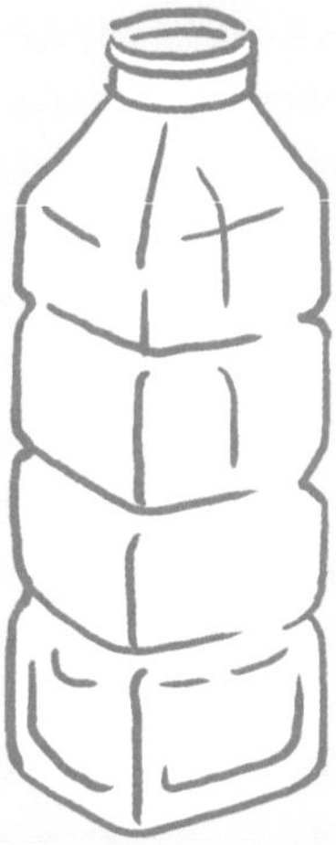

A large, empty drinks bottle

A bowl filled with hot water

A bowl filled with ice-cold water

REMOVE THE CAP FROM THE DRINKS BOTTLE AND PLACE THE BALLOON OVER THE TOP, MAKING SURE THE NECK OF THE BALLOON IS FULLY PULLED DOWN OVER THE NECK OF THE BOTTLE.

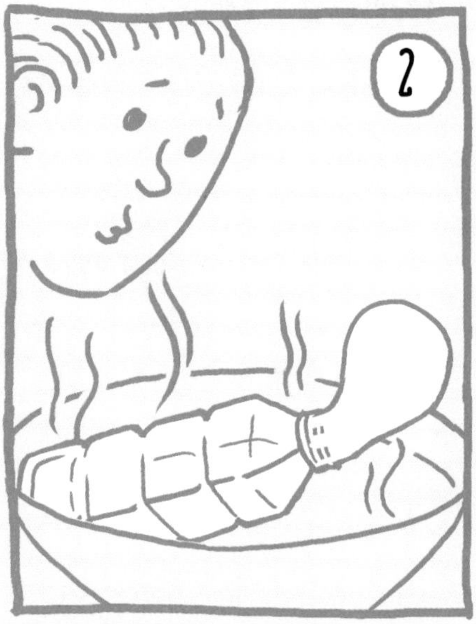

PLACE THE BOTTLE IN THE BOWL OF HOT WATER FOR A COUPLE OF MINUTES AND WATCH WHAT HAPPENS TO THE BALLOON!

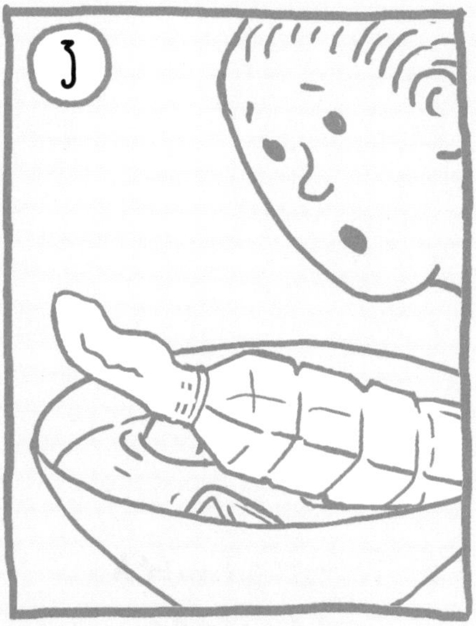

NOW PLACE IT IN THE COLD WATER. WATCH WHAT HAPPENS TO THE BALLOON!

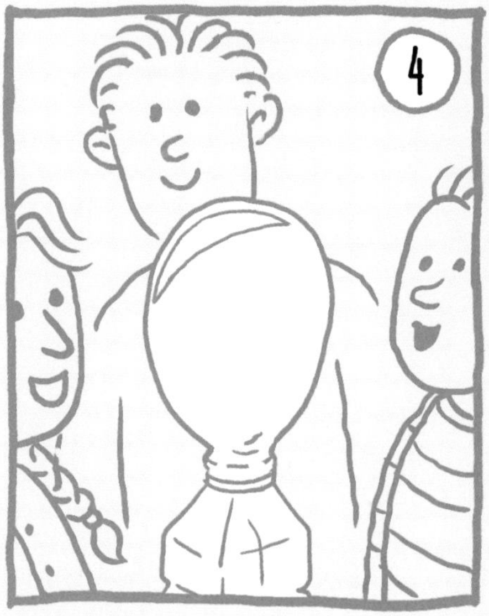

REPEAT AND WOW YOUR FRIENDS.

1

TOSS A COIN 20 TIMES AND SEE HOW MANY TIMES IT LANDS **UPSIDE DOWN** (THAT MEANS HEADS ON THE FLOOR AND TAILS IN THE AIR).

2

NOW TOSS A BUTTON 20 TIMES AND SEE HOW MANY TIMES IT LANDS **UPSIDE DOWN** (PICK WHICH SIDE IS 'UP' AND WHICH SIDE IS 'DOWN').

3

NEXT TOSS A BISCUIT IN THE AIR AND SEE IF IT LANDS **UPSIDE DOWN** IF IT DOES, EAT IT. IF IT DOESN'T, SEE HOW MANY THROWS IT TAKES BEFORE YOU CAN GET SCOFFING.

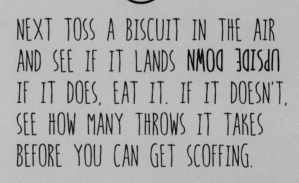

PRESENT YOUR FINDINGS IN THE SCIENTIFIC TABLE BELOW:

	LANDS UPSIDE DOWN	LANDS TOP SIDE UP
COIN		
BUTTON		
BISCUIT		

Join the dots and unscramble the words to

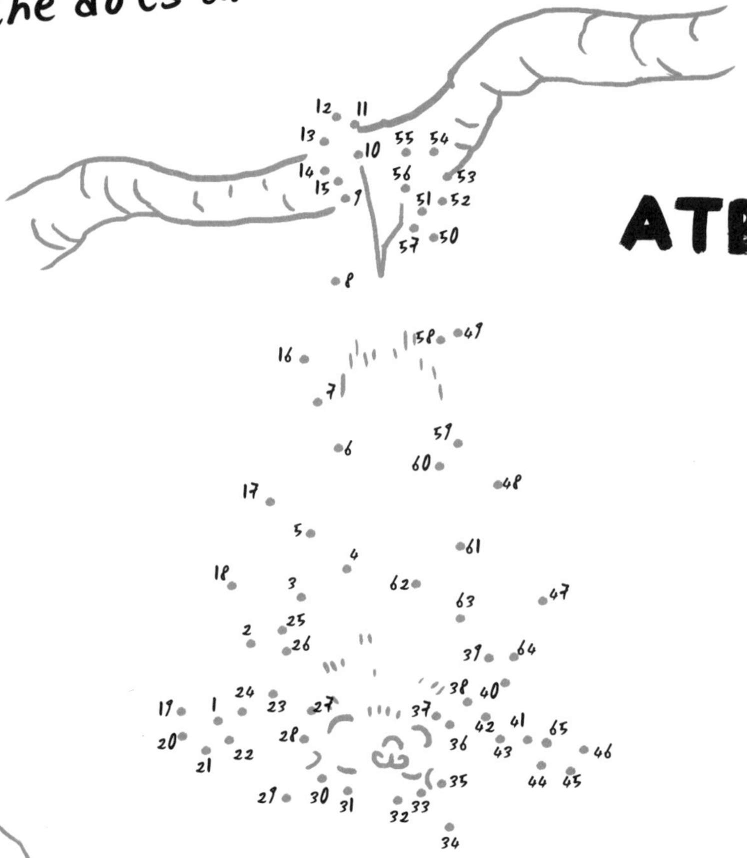

ATB

LTHOS

ANSWER: BAT, SLOTH, MANATEE

reveal three animals that sleep umop əpısdn.

TANAEME

GO OUTSIDE AND STICK WHAT'S ON THE GROUND IN THE AIR AND WHAT'S IN THE AIR ON THE GROUND.

Get a piece of clear sticky tape, stick it to the floor and peel it off. Stick it here.

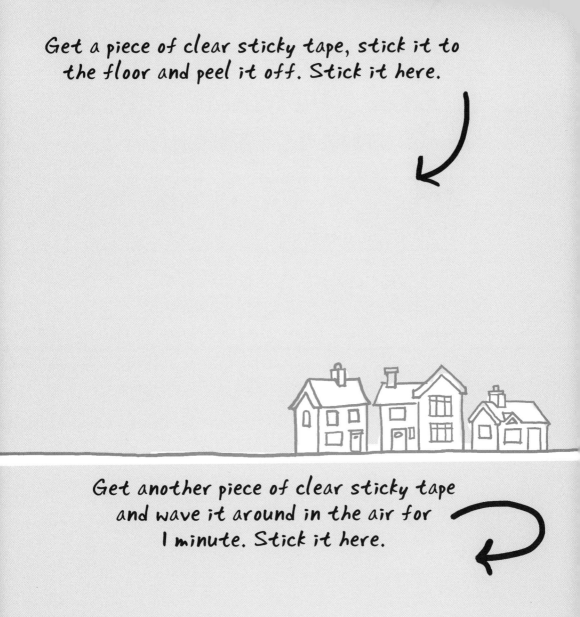

Get another piece of clear sticky tape and wave it around in the air for 1 minute. Stick it here.

DOODLE SOME FRUITS THAT LOOK THE SAME WHEN UPSIDE DOWN.

EAT A JAM DOUGHNUT INSIDE OUT. THAT MEANS LICKING OUT THE JAM BEFORE EATING ANY OF THE DOUGHNUT!

Create a backwards wordsearch for your friends!

① Put 10 words into the grid opposite but write them backwards. Fill in the empty squares with random letters.

② List out the words that need to be found and set your friend the challenge of finding them all within 5 minutes.

Like this!

DRAW YOUR DINNER USING THE LETTERS IN EACH FOOD'S NAME.

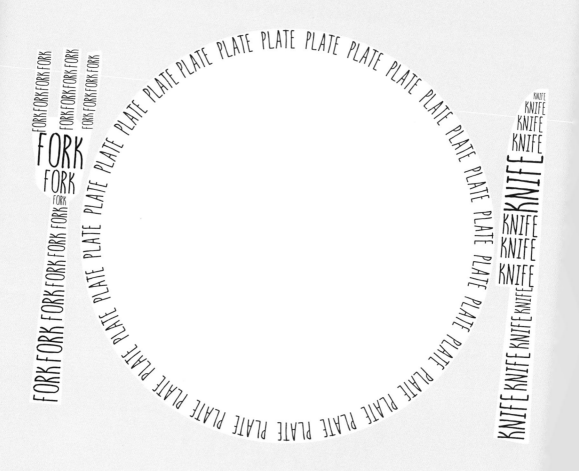

PLAY CATCH **UPSIDE DOWN** WITH A FRIEND BY THROWING AND CATCHING A BALL BETWEEN YOUR LEGS.

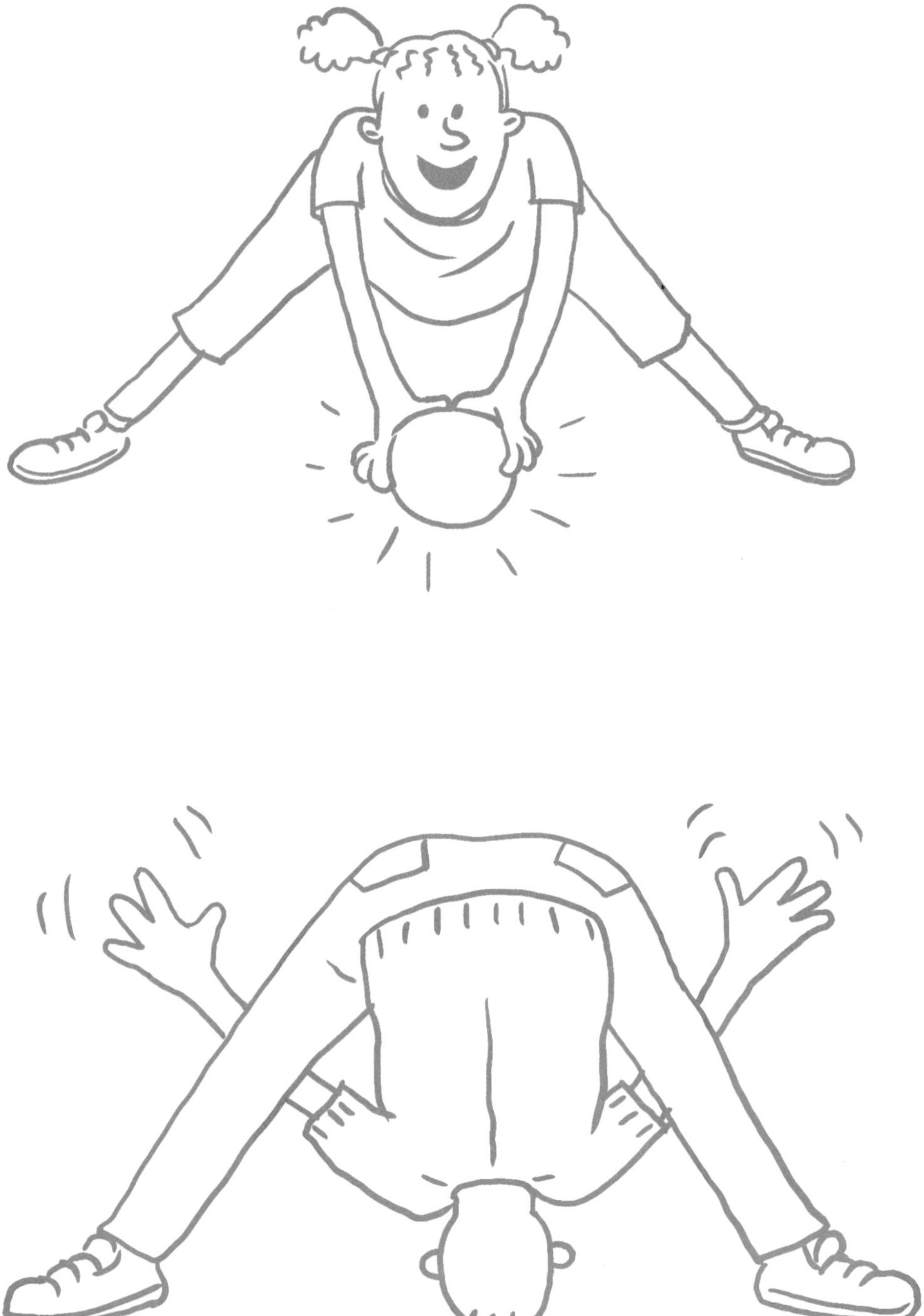

4. TURN THE KOOB SIDEWAYS.

5. ASK A FRIEND TO DRAW THE BOTTOM HALF OF THEIR FAVOURITE ANIMAL HERE.

6. FOLD THE PAGE IN HALF TO HIDE YOUR DRAWING.

1. TURN THE KOOB SIDEWAYS.

2. ASK A FRIEND TO DRAW THE TOP HALF OF THEIR FAVOURITE ANIMAL HERE.

3. FOLD THE PAGE IN HALF TO HIDE YOUR DRAWING.

7. OPEN OUT YOUR FOLDED PAGES TO REVEAL YOUR NEW ANIMAL.

GIVE IT A NAME!

....

DRAW AN UPSIDE-DOWN SELF-PORTRAIT HERE.

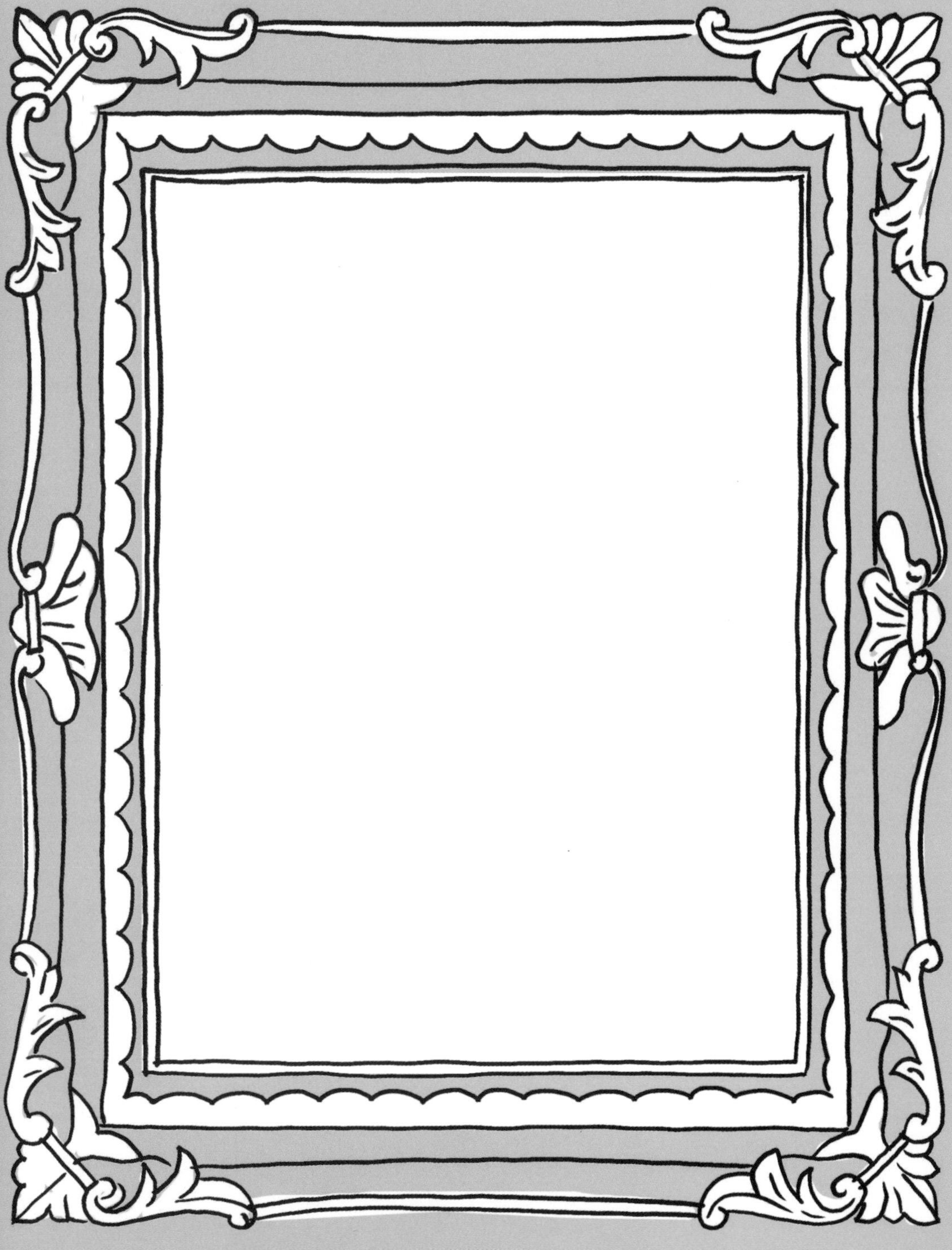

What has made these reflections in the water?

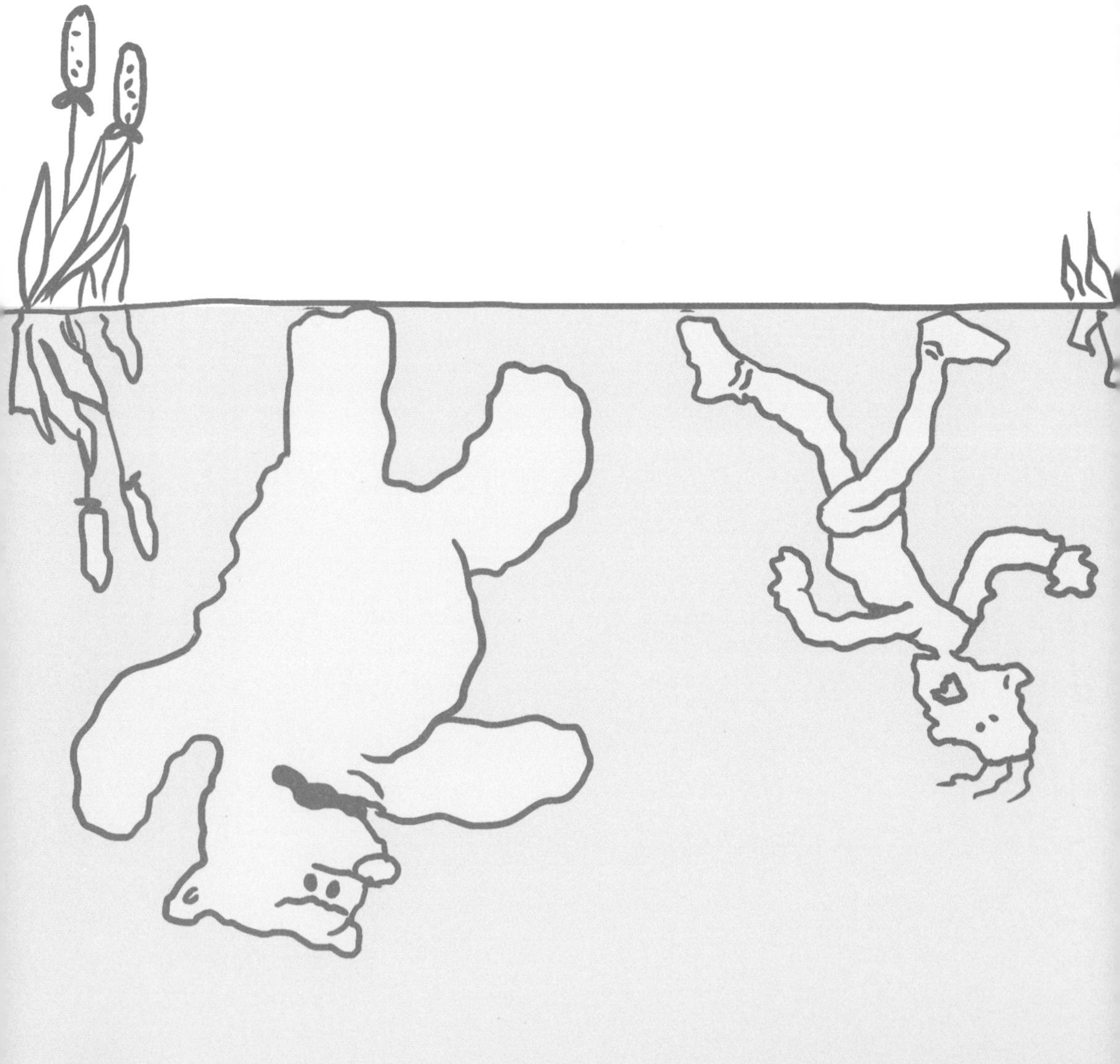

Draw them here.

Pass your body through this page!

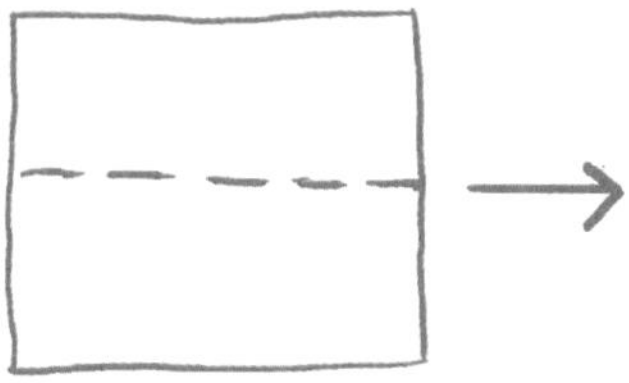

Cut the page out of the koob.

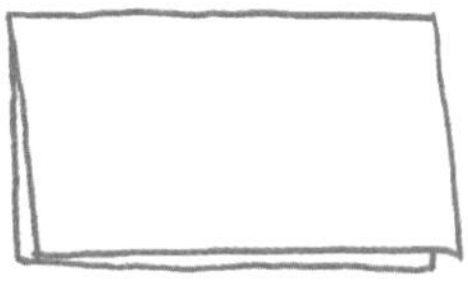

Fold the page in half vertically along dotted line.

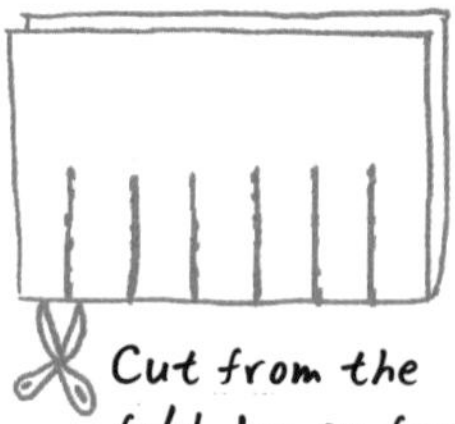

Cut from the fold, 1cm in from the edge, to 1cm from the end.

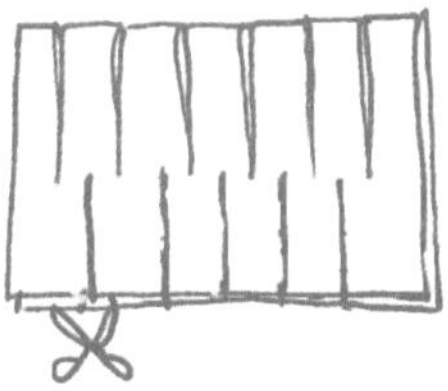

Turn the page around and cut in between the top cuts, like this.

You'll now have a double zigzag shape. Pull the two outer loops on the folded side away from the rest of the zigzag.

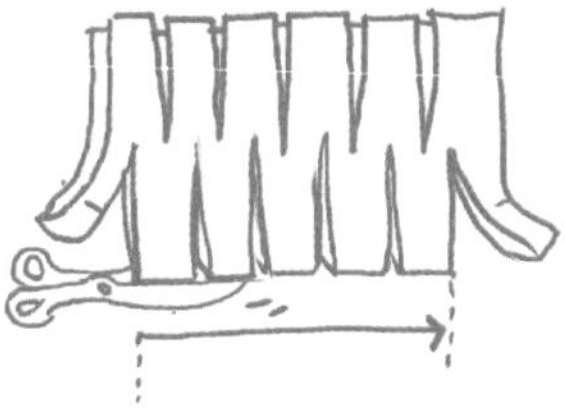

Cut through the folded edges of the middle strips, as shown.

Gently unfold the page into a huge open circle and impress your friends as you jump through it!

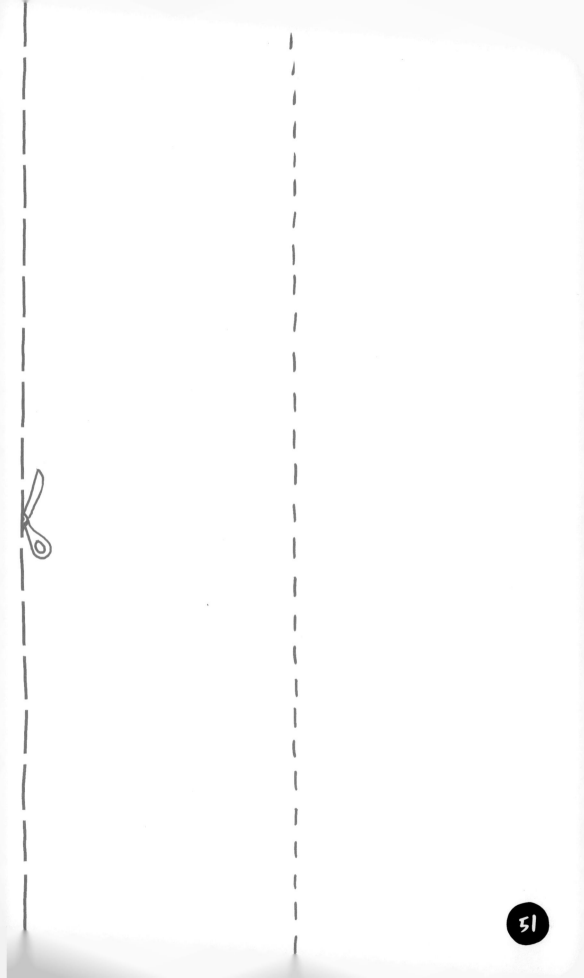

① CLOSE YOUR EYES AND DRAW A CLOCK ON THIS PAGE WITHOUT PEEKING. THE TIME IS 2:35.

② THEN, WITH YOUR EYES STILL CLOSED, TURN THE PAGE UPSIDE DOWN AND REDRAW THE NUMBERS AROUND THE EDGE OF THE CLOCK FACE SO THE HANDS NOW SHOW THE TIME AS 8:05.

③ OPEN YOUR EYES AND SEE WHAT TIMES YOU ACTUALLY DREW!

WHERE DO PEOPLE LIVE UPSIDE DOWN?

...IN SPACE!

COVER YOUR HAND IN PAINT, INK OR TOMATO SAUCE. MAKE AN UPSIDE-DOWN HANDPRINT HERE. →

BUT WHICH WAY IS UPSIDE DOWN?

IS YOUR PALM THE TOP OR THE BOTTOM OF A HANDPRINT?? ARE YOUR FINGERS AT THE BEGINNING OR THE END OF YOUR HAND??

PUZZLING!

1 FILL A TRAY WITH 10 ITEMS.

2 ASK A FRIEND TO LOOK AT THE TRAY FOR 10 SECONDS.

3 COVER THE TRAY AND THE ITEMS WITH A TEA TOWEL.

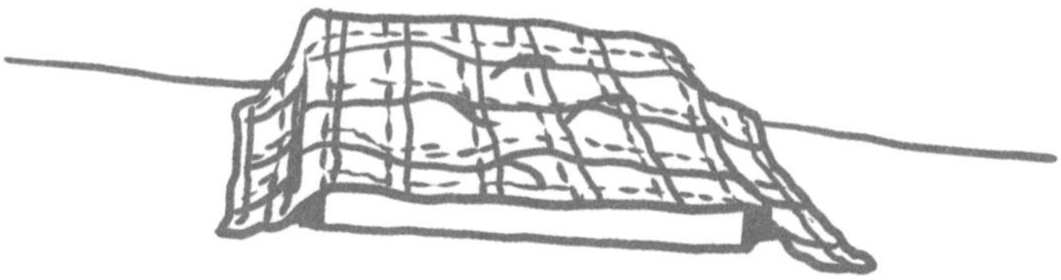

④

ASK THE FRIEND TO LOOK AWAY WHILE YOU TURN ONE OBJECT ON THE TRAY NMOꓷ ƎꓷISԀꓵ.

⑤

SHOW YOUR FRIEND THE TRAY AGAIN AND REMOVE THE TEA TOWEL. CAN THEY SPOT THE OBJECT THAT IS NOW NMOꓷ ƎꓷISԀꓵ?

Tips and tricks to make the game harder:

- pick objects that look similar umop ǝpᴉsdn, such as a coin.
- fill the tray with 10 pencils all with their ends pointing in different directions, turn one pencil umop ǝpᴉsdn.
- don't turn any of the items but hold the tray with your hands umop ǝpᴉsdn!

TEAR OUT THE OPPOSITE PAGE.

TAPE IT TO THE UNDERNEATH OF YOUR KITCHEN TABLE.

SIT ON THE FLOOR AND DRAW WHAT IS ON TOP OF THE TABLE ON THE PIECE OF PAPER.

YOUR DINNER IS NOW SERVED UPSIDE DOWN!

DRAW A SPIRAL ON THIS PAGE THAT LOOKS THE SAME UPSIDE DOWN, SIDEWAYS AND BACK TO FRONT. YOU CAN USE A MIRROR TO CHECK ITS REFLECTION.

Turn a glass of water uʍop ǝpısdn!

What you need:

A glass

Water

A page from this koob

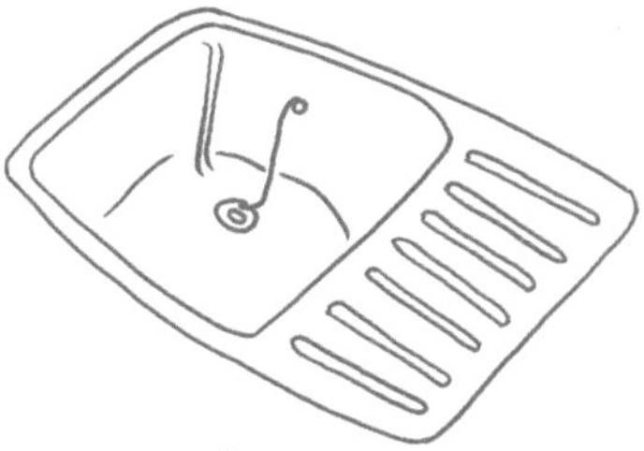

A sink

What you do:

1. Cut the opposite page out of the koob.

2. Fill the glass up to the top with water.

3. Place the page over the glass.

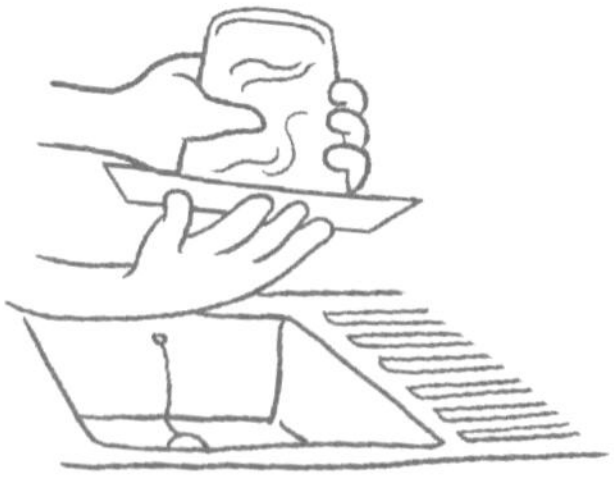

4. Quickly turn the glass uʍop ǝpısdn over a sink while holding the page in position.

5. Remove your hand from the page – the glass of water is now ¡uʍop ǝpısdn

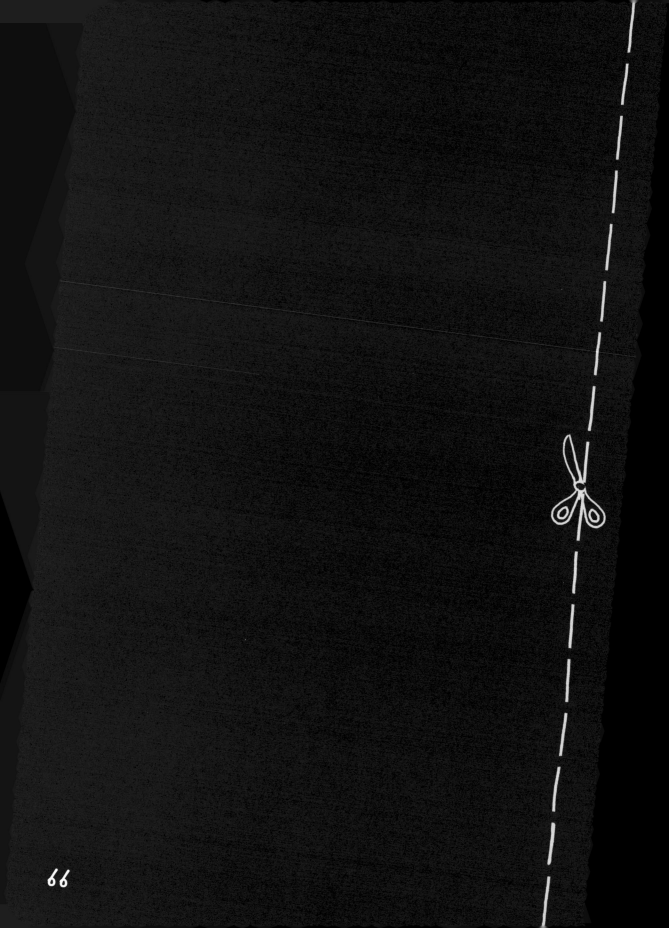

HOW MANY TIMES CAN YOU WRITE THE WORDS 'UPSIDE DOWN' IN THIS BOX?

I GUESS ………………… TIMES

I ACTUALLY WROTE IT ………………… TIMES.

HOW MANY OF THESE UPSIDE-DOWN COUNTRIES CAN YOU NAME?

A.

B.

C.

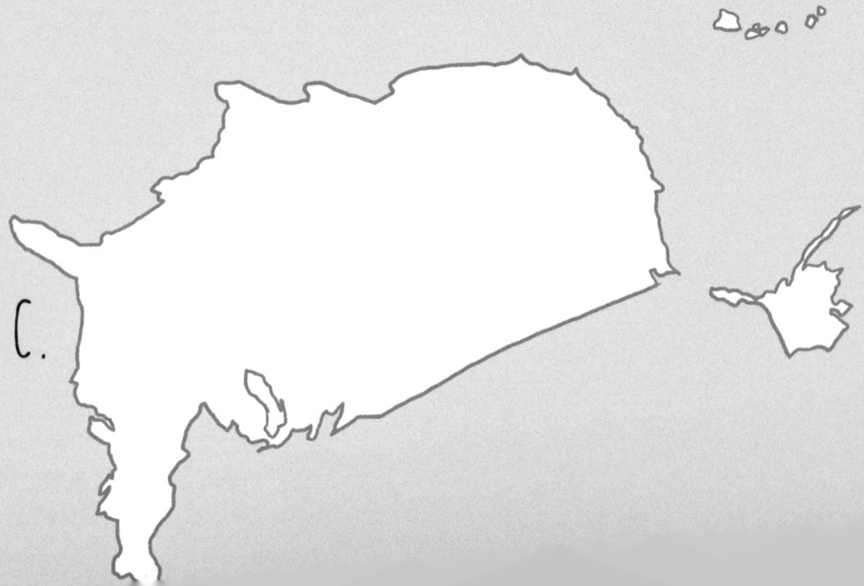

D.

E.

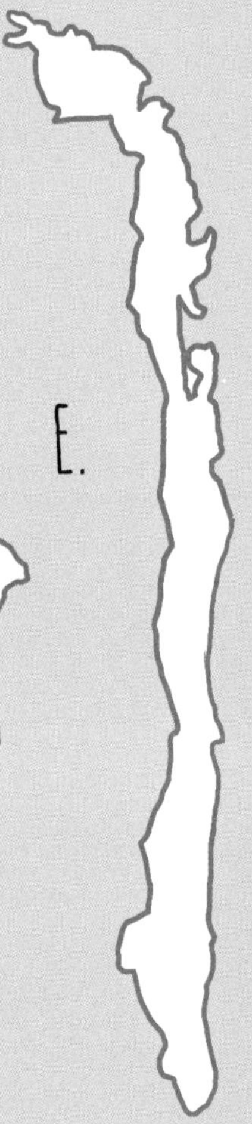

F.

ANSWERS: A. UNITED KINGDOM, B. ITALY, C. USA, D. AUSTRALIA, E. CHILE, F. RUSSIA

Draw an object uʍop ǝpᴉsdn and think of a new use for it.

An umbrella used uʍop ǝpᴉsdn is a duck pond.

An uʍop ǝpᴉsdn candle
becomes a rocket booster.

A floor lamp used
uʍop ǝpᴉsdn is a coat rack.

Ask an adult to help you bake an uʍop-ǝpısdn cake!

Ingredients for the topping:

50 g
softened butter

50 g light
brown sugar

7–10 pineapple rings in syrup

7–10 glacé cherries

Ingredients for the cake:

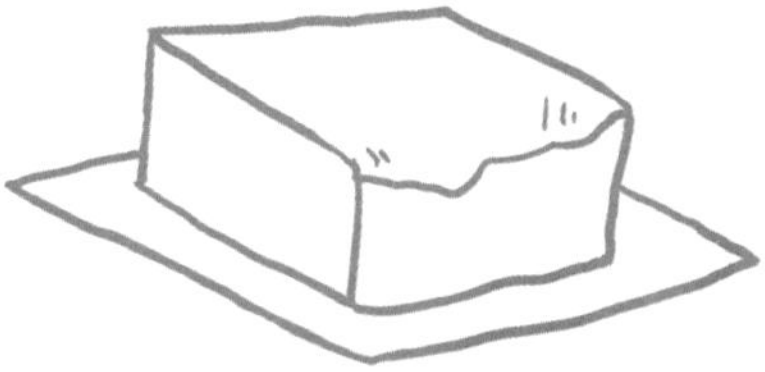

100 g
softened butter

2 eggs

100 g
caster sugar

100 g
self-raising flour

1 teaspoon baking powder

1 teaspoon
vanilla extract

2 tablespoons pineapple
syrup from the rings

1. Preheat the oven to 180°C.

2. To make the topping, beat the butter and sugar together until creamy.

3. Grab a 20-cm cake tin and spread the butter mix over the base and halfway up the sides. Try not to eat it all at this stage!

4. Arrange the pineapple rings on top of the butter mix and place a cherry in the centre of each ring.

5. To make the cake, beat all the ingredients together with 2 tablespoons of the pineapple syrup. Work those arm muscles!

6. Spoon the mix into the cake tin, on top of the pineapple, and smooth out.

7. Bake in the oven for 35 minutes. Ask an adult to help you use the oven.

8. Once cooked, leave to stand for 5 minutes then turn out onto a plate. Your uʍop-ǝpısdn cake is ready to eat!

WHAT GOES UP MUST COME DOWN.

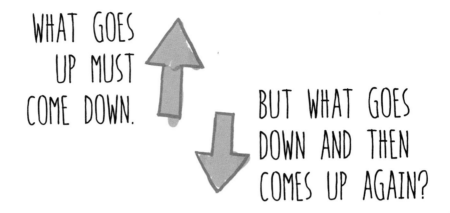

BUT WHAT GOES DOWN AND THEN COMES UP AGAIN?

NEED A CLUE OR TWO?

1. THERE ARE FOUR LETTERS IN THIS OBJECT'S NAME, BUT ONLY TWO LETTERS OF THE ALPHABET.

2. IT IS ATTACHED TO A PIECE OF STRING.

DRAW IT HERE:

ANSWER: A YO-YO!

WHAT'S MADE FROM WATER AND MINERALS AND GROWS DOWN?

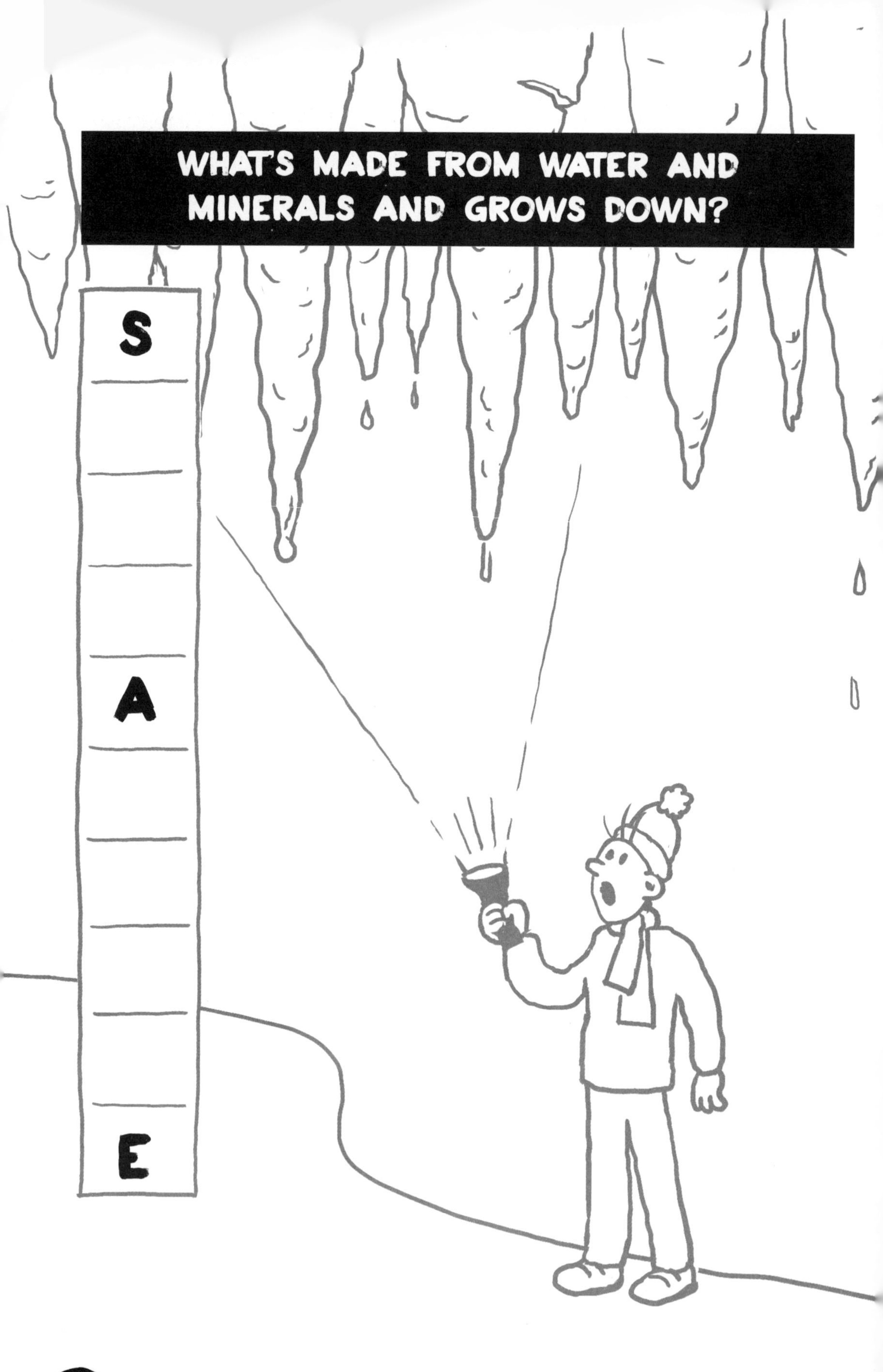

ANSWER: STALACTITE

WHAT'S MADE FROM WATER AND MINERALS AND GROWS UP?

HINT: WRITE THIS ONE FROM THE BOTTOM UP!

GRAB YOUR PENCILS AND COLOUR IN THIS CAVE. THE MINERALS MAKE THE ROCKS MULTICOLOURED.

ANSWER: STALAGMITE

Spell your family's names backwards.
Who has the best eman? For example:

Dom = Mod

Emma = Amme

Rachel = Lehcar

Toby = Ybot

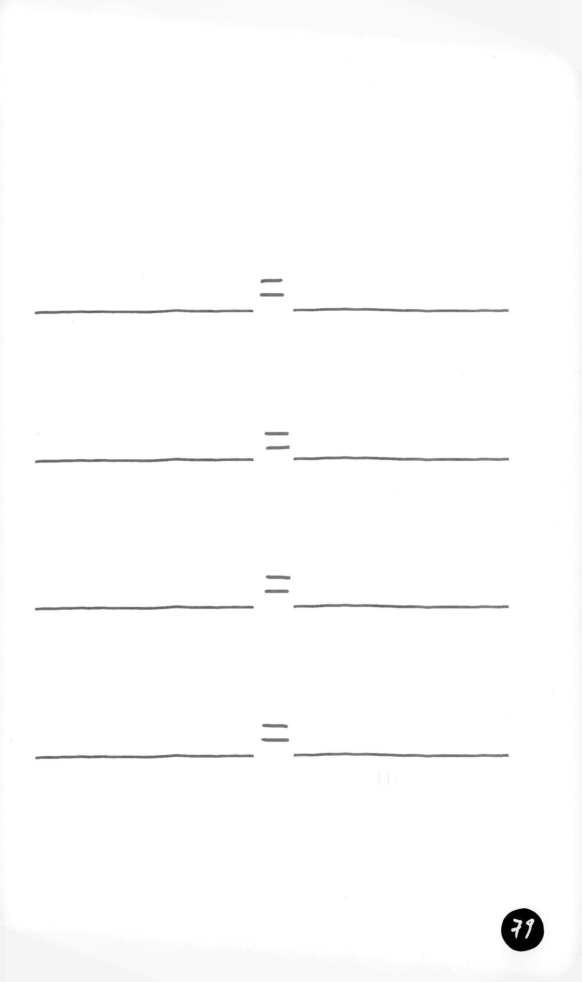

TAPE A LINE OF MASKING TAPE ALONG THE FLOOR...

IMAGINE IT'S A TIGHTROPE AND WALK BACKWARDS ALONG IT.

DON'T. FALL. OFF.

How many pieces can you cut this page of the koob into?

I guess:

_ _ _ _ .

Actual total:

_ _ _ _ .

Stick some of the pieces here:

DRAW THE BUMS ON THESE DUCKS HAVING AN UPSIDE-DOWN DUNK.

Help Eddie the electric eel get through the metal maze without touching the sides and getting a shock.

Finish

THIS IS THE UPSIDE-DOWN KINGDOM WHERE KING TOM RULES.

DESIGN A FLAG FOR THIS UPSIDE-DOWN LAND.

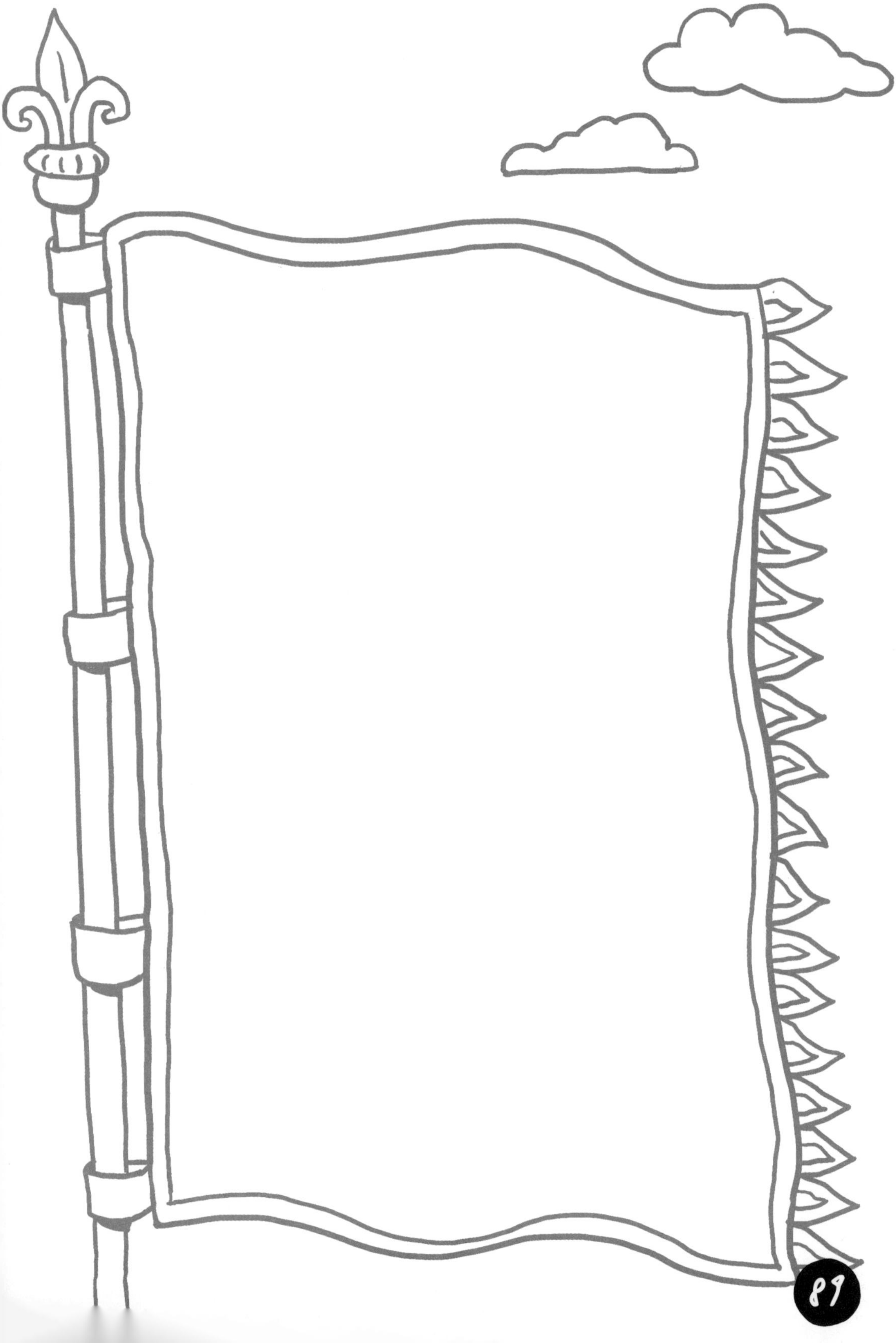

WOꞱ ⅁NIꓘ needs a new crown.
It must be uʍop ǝpısdn of course.
Cut this one out and colour it in.

Instructions:

① Cut out the three shapes on the next page.

② Draw on a design and colour it in, making sure any jewels are uʍop ǝpısdn.

③ Stick tab A to area B, tab C to area D and tab E to area F.

④ Try out sˌɯoꞱ ƃuıꓘ crown for size – adjust the length of the strips at the back of the crown to your head.

⑤ Wear it uʍop ǝpısdn of course!

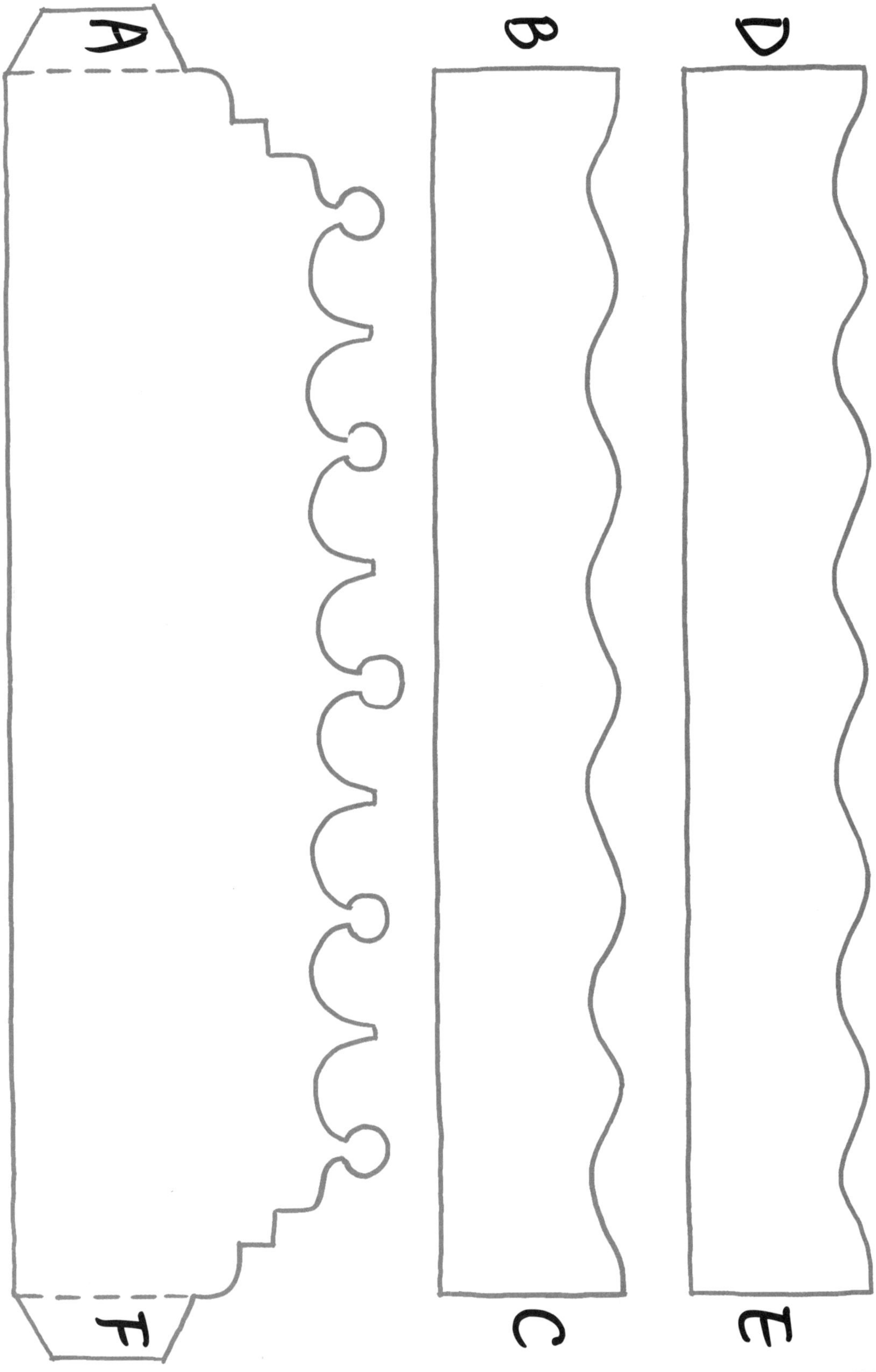
A
B
C
D
E
F

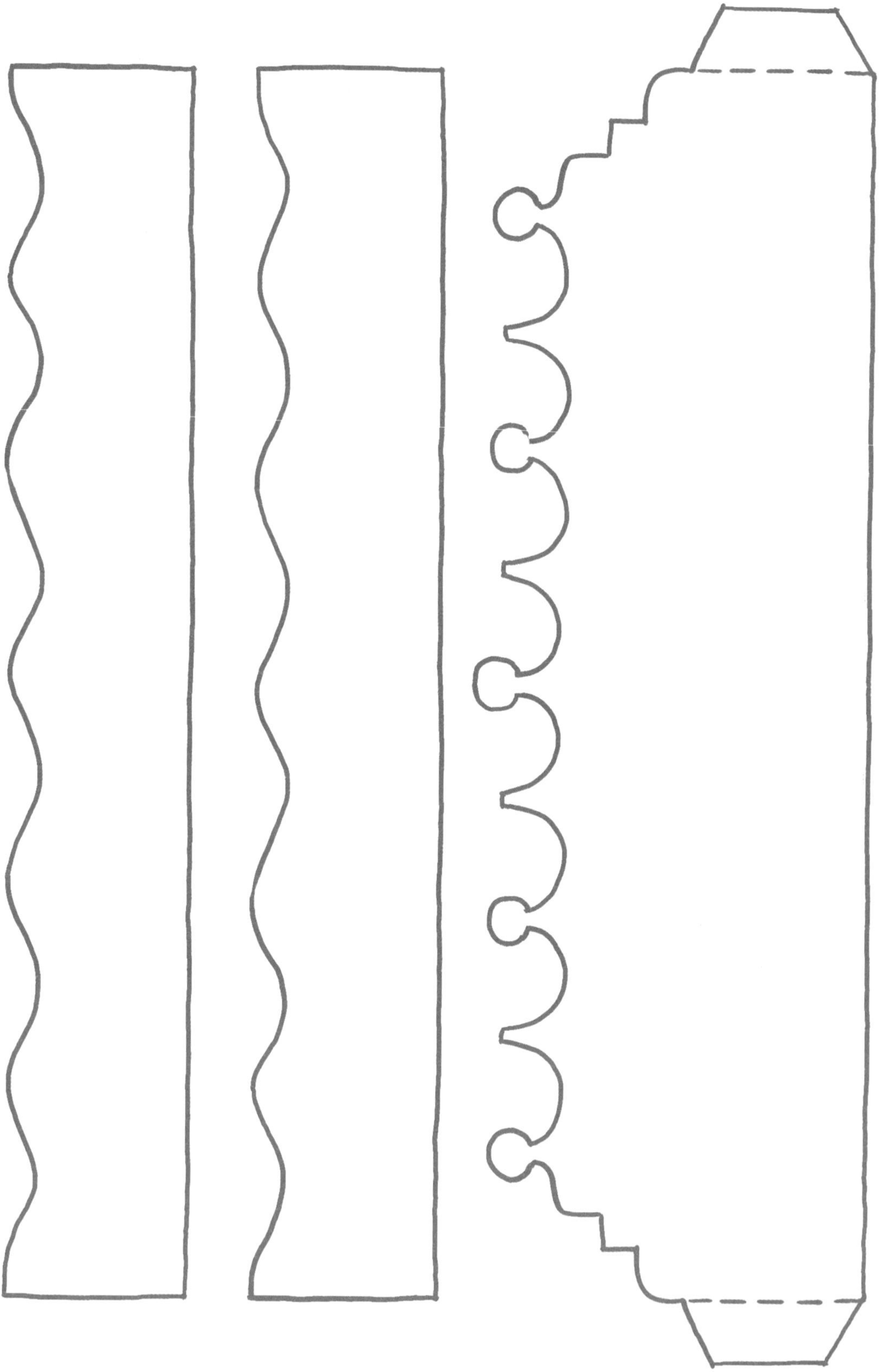

FILL THIS PAGE WITH UPSIDE-DOWN QUESTION MARKS.
WHY? WHY NOT!

WOꞱ ⅁NIꓘ not only lives in an uʍop-ǝpısdn kingdom, he lives in an uʍop-ǝpısdn palace. The bedrooms are in the basement, the chairs are on the ceiling, the lights are on in the day and off at night and the chef serves unbaked cakes.

Doodle in a day of uʍop-ǝpısdn palace life here.

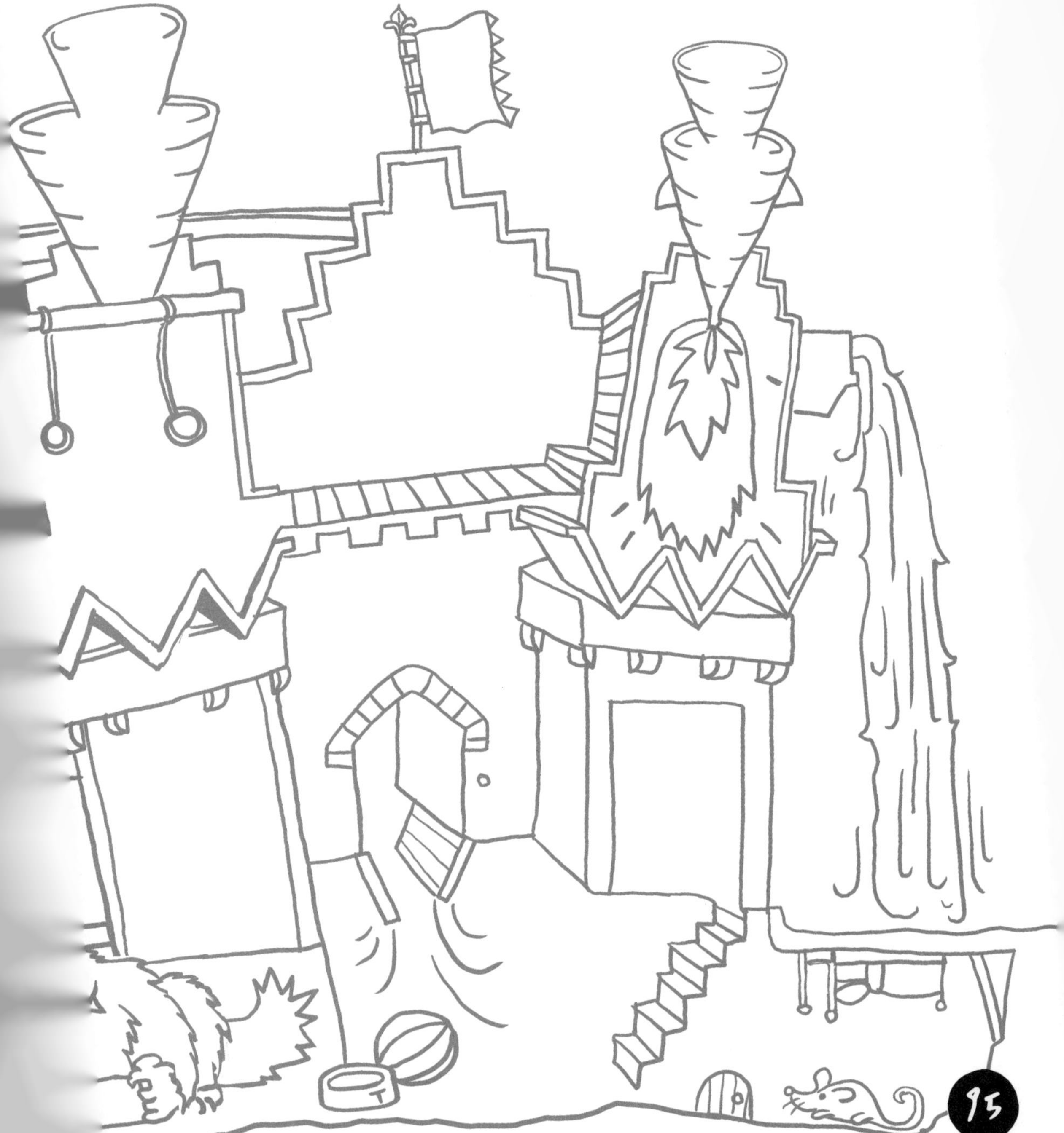

Play pass the parcel backwards.

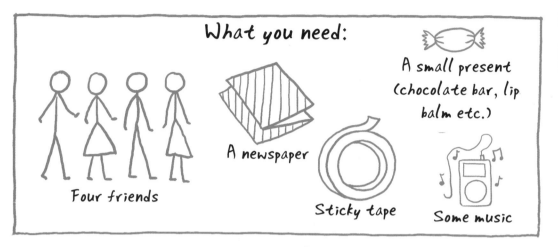

What you need:

Four friends

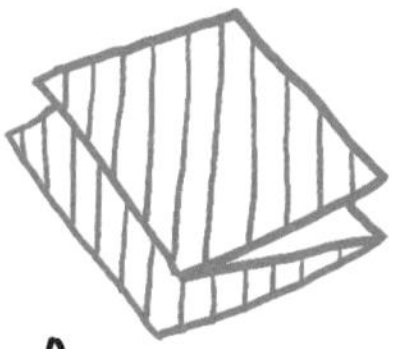

A newspaper

A small present (chocolate bar, lip balm etc.)

Sticky tape

Some music

How to play:

Before your friends arrive you need to wrap up the gift in newspaper.

Ask an adult or sibling to be your DJ for the game.

Once you're ready to play, simply sit in a circle and pass the gift around to the beat of the music.

You DJ should stop the music roughly every 20 seconds. Whoever is holding the gift at that time has to add another layer of newspaper wrapping to the gift.

Keep playing for 10 minutes and see how many layers of wrapping you can put on the gift.

Once 10 minutes are up, the DJ must close their eyes and stop the music when-ever they wish.

Whoever is holding the gift at this stage has to try to unwrap it in 30 seconds. If they don't do it in time, the gift passes to the person on the right who has a another 30 seconds to try to unwrap it.

Keep going until the gift is finally unwrapped!

CATCH SOME AIR, KICKFLIP THE BOARD, OLLIE OVER YOUR DOG AND PULL A 360!

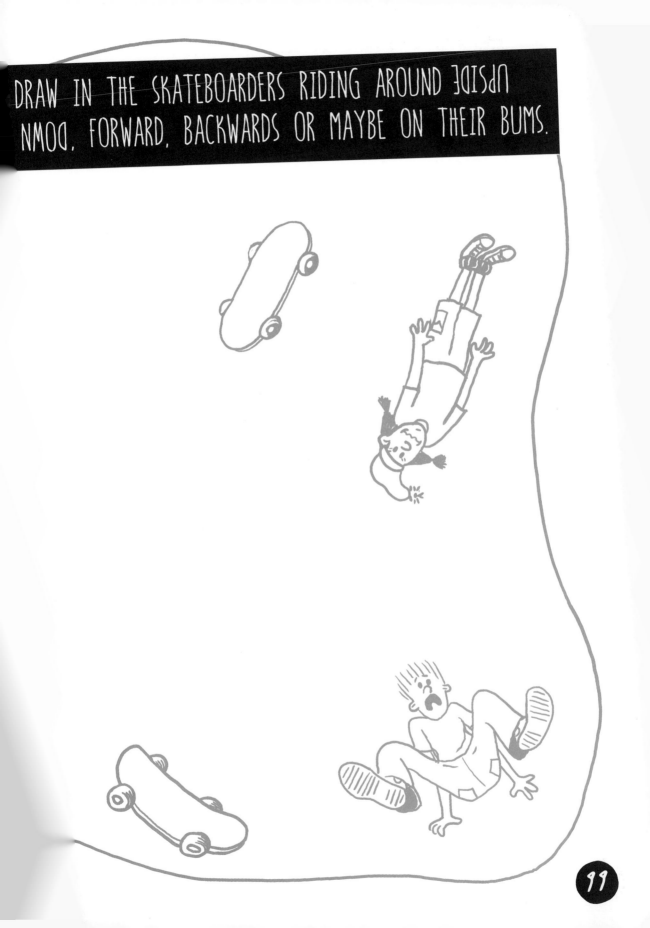

DRAW IN THE SKATEBOARDERS RIDING AROUND UPSIDE DOWN, FORWARD, BACKWARDS OR MAYBE ON THEIR BUMS.

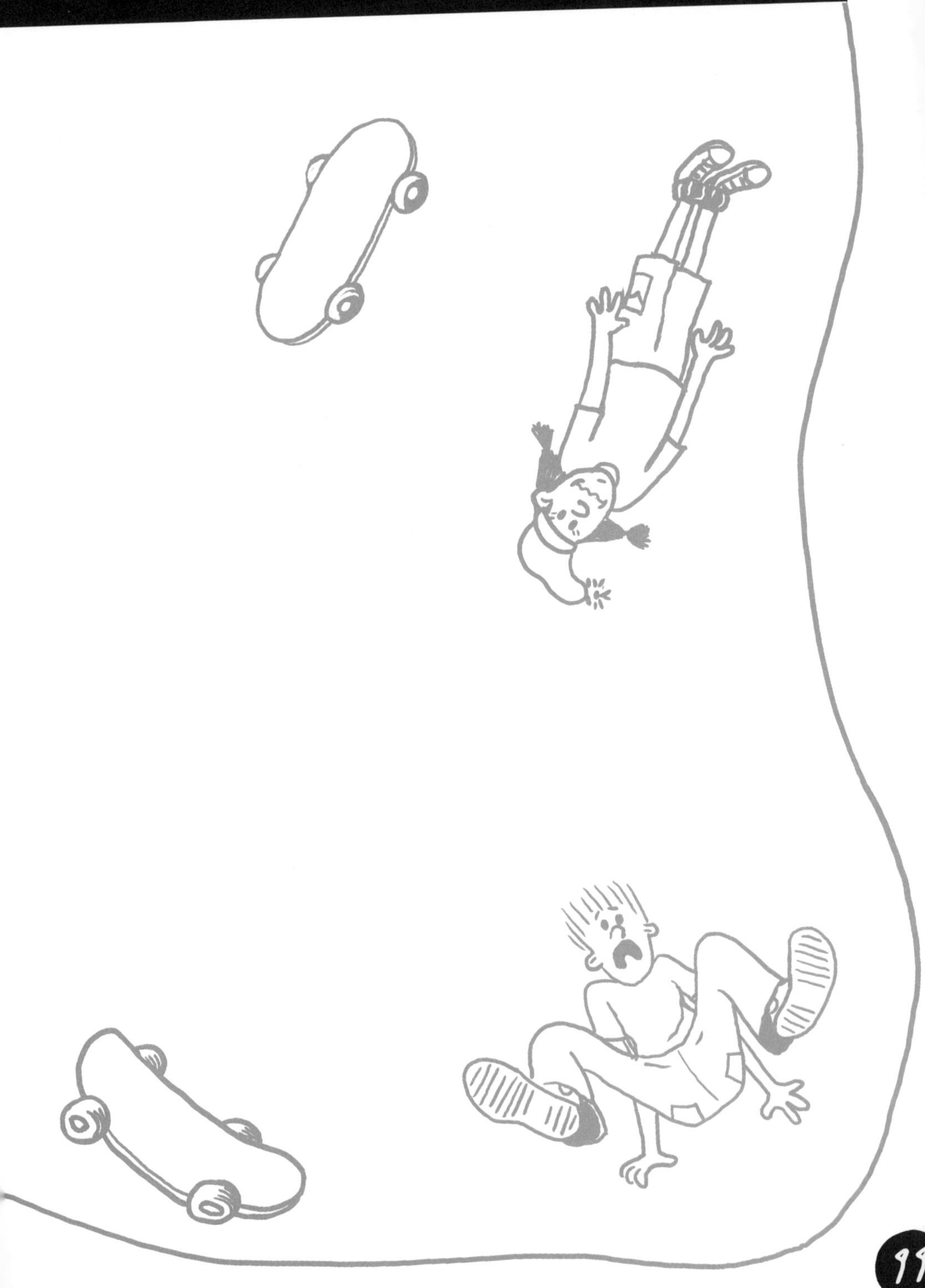

Circle a paragraph of writing in your favourite magazine.
Rewrite it on this page and switch around all the 'L's and 'R's.
"Now lead it out roud in a posh voice."

DRESS UPSIDE DOWN FOR THE DAY. THAT MEANS PANTS ON YOUR HEAD, TROUSERS LIKE A SCARF AND A T-SHIRT AS A SKIRT.

IF ANYONE ASKS WHY YOU'RE DOING THIS, JUST SAY YOU'RE DRESSING LIKE YOUR COUSIN WHO LIVES UPSIDE DOWN ON THE OTHER SIDE OF THE WORLD.

Salutations, readers.
We introduce you to the new
art of koob yoga.

Try to balance the book somewhere on your body when doing these moves. Here are your poses, yogi students.

MASH-UP SOME INSECT TOPS AND MAMMAL BOTTOMS.

NAME YOUR TOPSY-TURVY ANIMAL CREATIONS.

Layer some liquids!

What you need:

How to do it:

Pour enough honey into the bottom of the bottle to form a layer.

Squirt washing up liquid on top of the honey so it forms a layer.

Put a few drops of red food colouring into a glass of water, then pour it on top of the washing-up liquid.

Finally pour a layer of vegetable oil into the bottle.

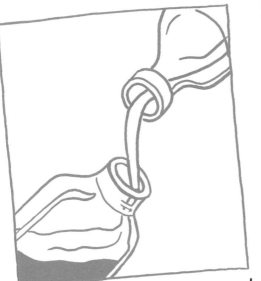

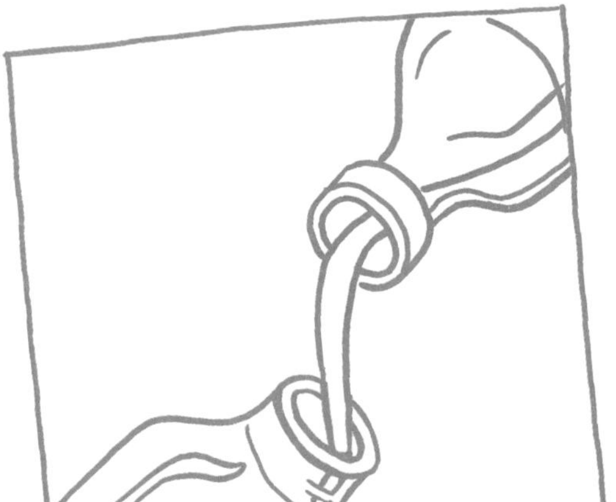

Turn the bottle uʍop ǝpısdn, leave it to settle for a minute or two.

Your liquid layers are permanent!

Make a bridge to cross from this page to page 113. How? Just follow the instructions below of course!

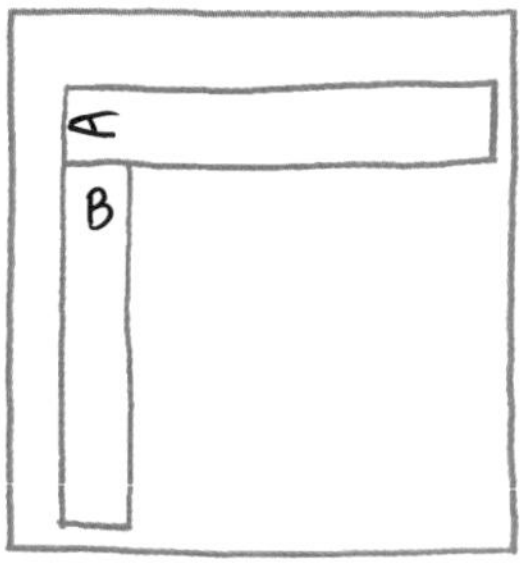

Cut out the two strips. Glue the ends of A and B together as shown. Strip B should sit on top of strip A.

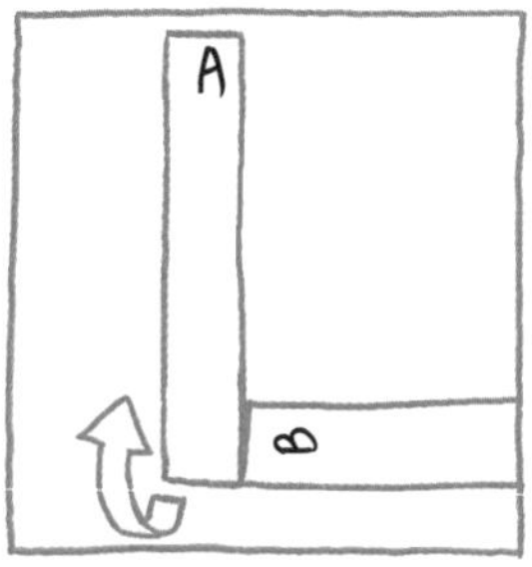

Fold strip A up and over strip B.

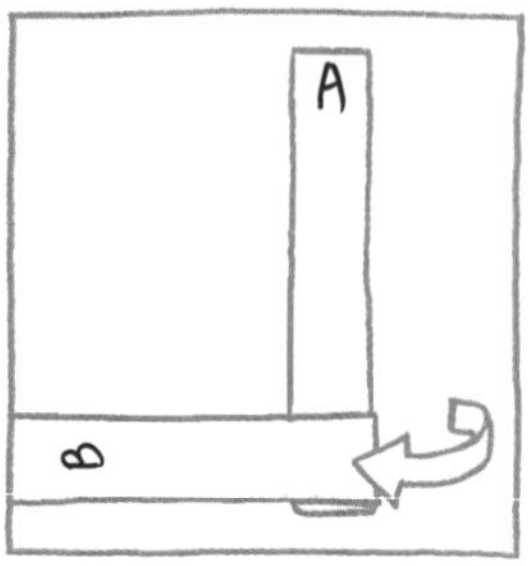

Now fold strip B over strip A.

Continue like this until you've used up the entire strips of paper.

Stick the two ends together.

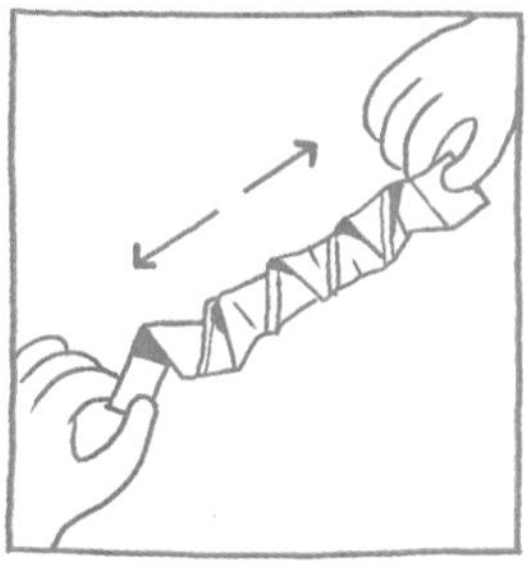

Gently pull the ends away from each other to stretch out your zigzag bridge.

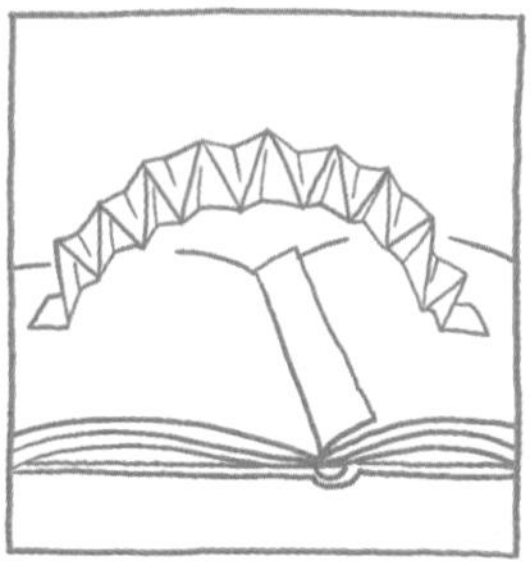

Stick one end to page 110 and the other end to page 113. You've made a bridge from one page to the other!

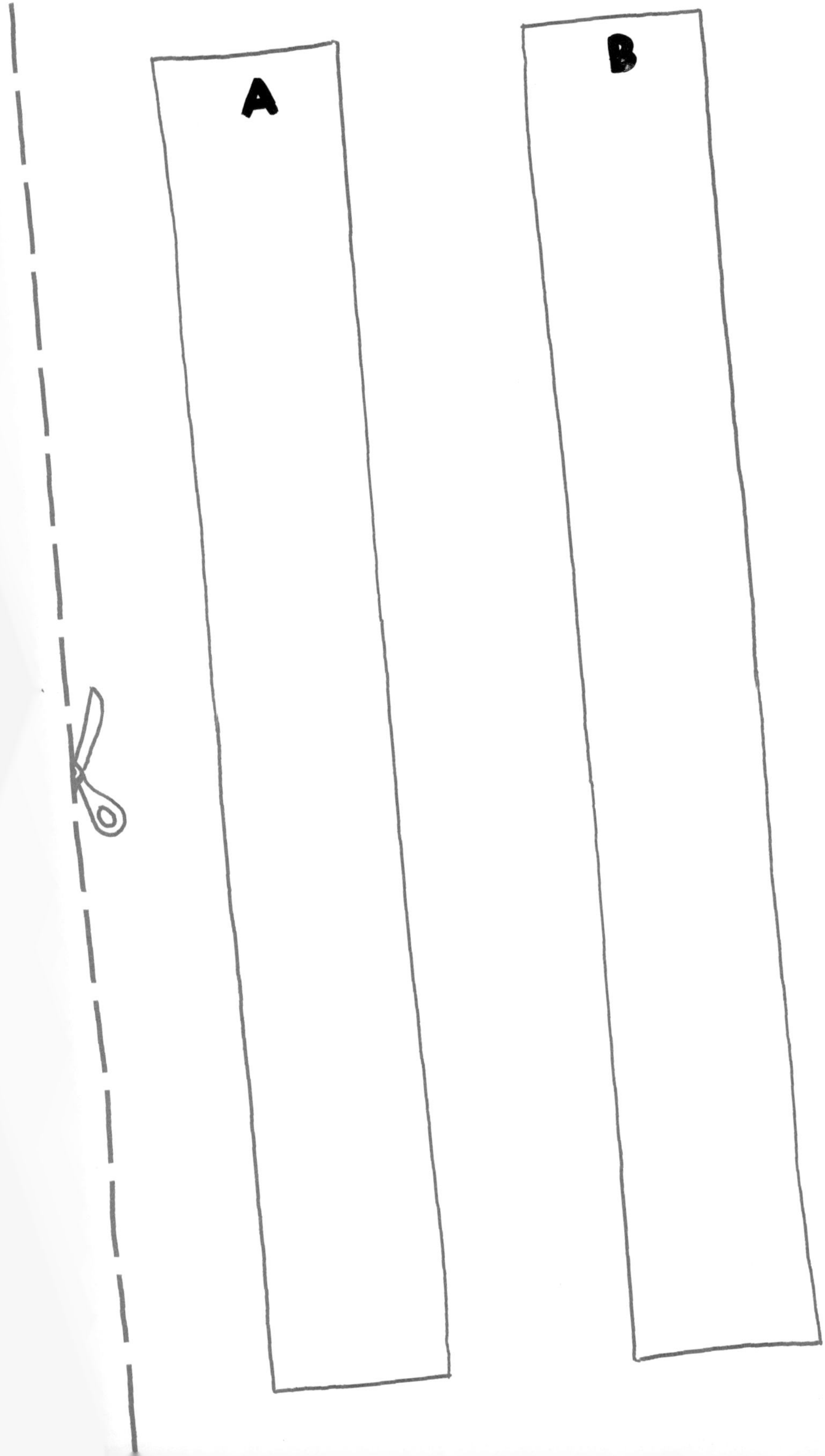
A
B

HOLD A WEAK MAN COMPETITION WITH YOUR FRIENDS.

HOW LITTLE CAN YOU LIFT?
AWARD A PRIZE TO THE WINNER.

WHAT WOULD THE WORLD BE LIKE IF CATS AND DOGS WERE REPLACED WITH EXTINCT DODOS AND SABRETOOTH TIGERS?

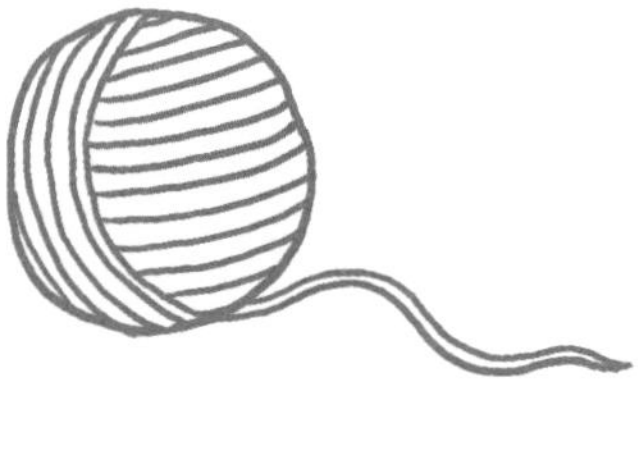

WRAP THIS PAGE IN TOILET PAPER.

THE KOOB IS NOW READY FOR ANY BATHROOM EMERGENCY!

Sleep uʍop ǝpısdn tonight. That means:

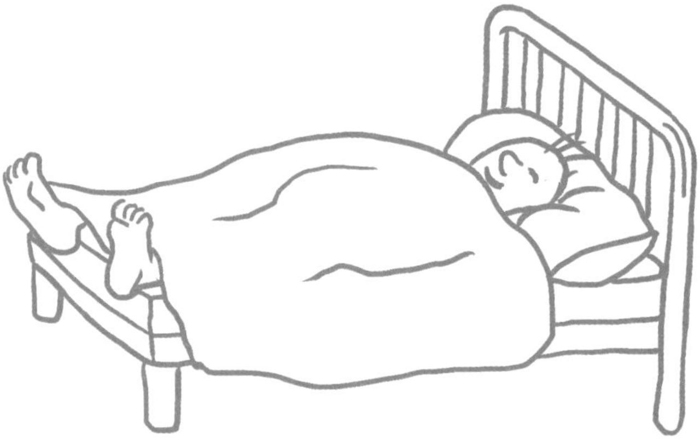

① LYING ON YOUR BACK (IF YOU NORMALLY SLEEP ON YOUR FRONT).

② LYING ON YOUR FRONT (IF YOU NORMALLY SLEEP ON YOUR BACK).

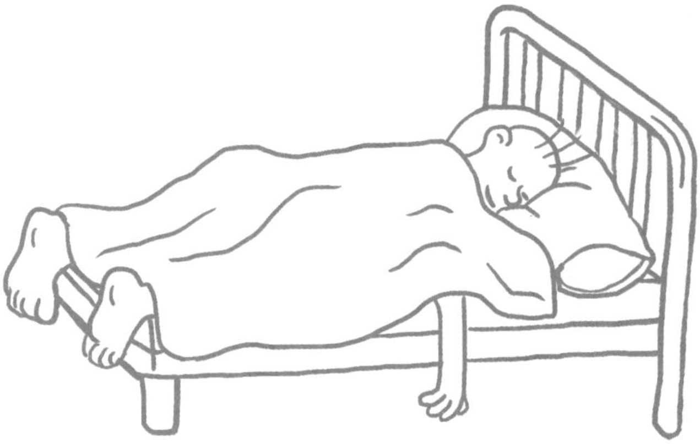

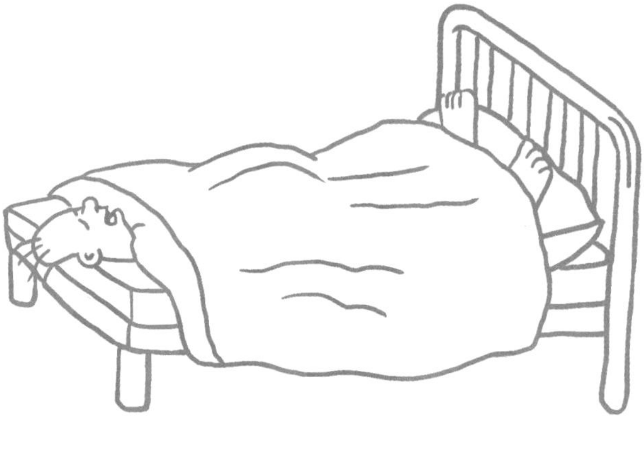

③ SLEEPING WITH YOUR HEAD AT THE OPPOSITE END OF THE BED (YOU COULD EVEN GIVE YOUR FEET THE PILLOW FOR A CHANGE).

A MAN THROWS A BALL, AND IT TRAVELS 1 METRE AND THEN COMES BACK TO HIM AND HE EASILY CATCHES IT. IT DOESN'T HIT ANYTHING, IT'S NOT A BOOMERANG-SHAPED BALL AND NO ONE ELSE IS AROUND TO THROW IT TO HIM. SO HOW DOES THIS HAPPEN?

CLUE: YOU'LL NEED TO TURN YOUR BRAIN 90 DEGREES TO WORK THIS ONE OUT.

ANSWER: HE THROWS IT UP IN THE AIR!

RENAME THE EVEN NUMBERS IN THIS LIST. USE ANY EXISTING WORDS YOU WANT, OR MAKE UP A WORD. MEMORIZE THE NAMES AND THEN USE THEM INSTEAD OF SAYING OR WRITING DOWN THOSE NUMBERS FOR A DAY.

---

1. ONE
2. ....
3. THREE
4. ....
5. FIVE

NOTE: WE TAKE NO RESPONSIBILITY FOR THE ANGER OF YOUR MATHS TEACHER!

6. ....

7. SEVEN

8. ....

9. NINE

10. ....

Ever heard the phrase "You live in a bubble"? Now you really can fit in a bubble!

What you need:

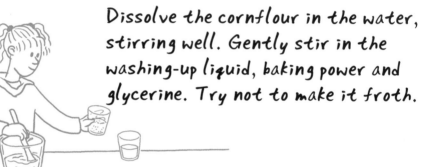

Dissolve the cornflour in the water, stirring well. Gently stir in the washing-up liquid, baking power and glycerine. Try not to make it froth.

Allow the mixture to sit for an hour.

Meanwhile, make your bubble blower. Thread the string through two straws then tie the ends together. Move the knot so it's inside one of the straws.

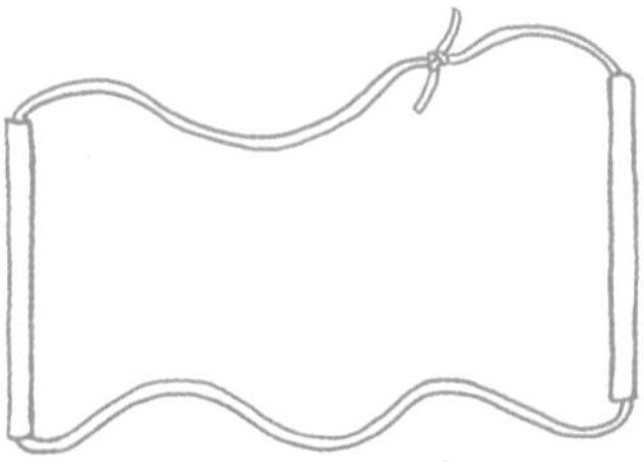

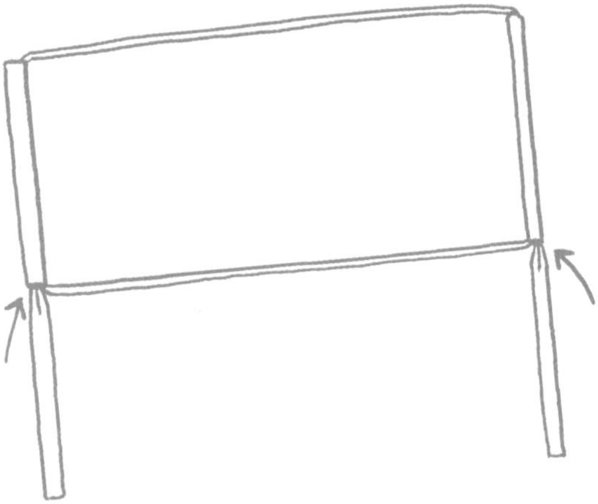

Push the other two straws inside the straws on the string to make handles.

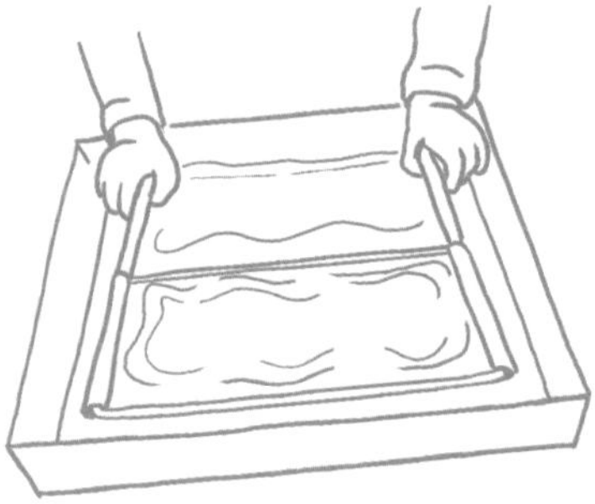

Pour your bubble mix into a wide, shallow container.

Dunk the string and straw loop into the bubble mix by holding onto the straw handles, then gently lift it out. Move the handles away from each other so the string becomes taught.

Hold the loop in the air, moving it gently and your bubble should form. Try to get a person inside your bubble!

LEAVE A BUBBLE PRINT ON THESE PAGES.

POP!

THIS SUBMARINE HAS VENTURED TO THE VERY BOTTOM OF THE DEEPEST OCEAN. DOODLE WHAT LIVES IN THE DEPTHS. IF THE SUB KEEPS TRAVELLING, WHAT DO YOU THINK IT'LL FIND NEXT? WILL IT POP OUT OF THE OCEAN ON THE OPPOSITE SIDE OF THE WORLD?

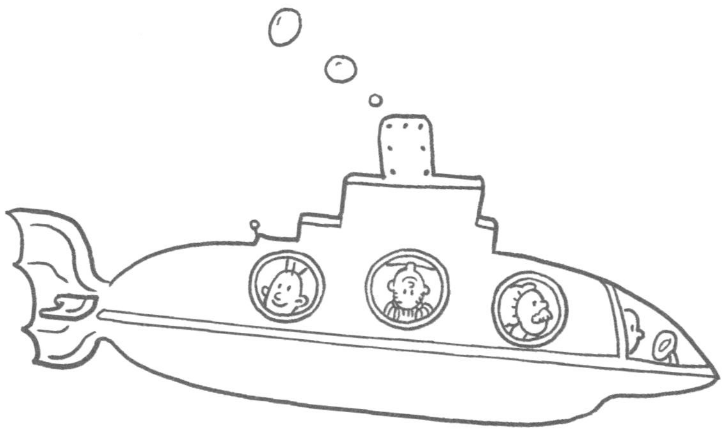

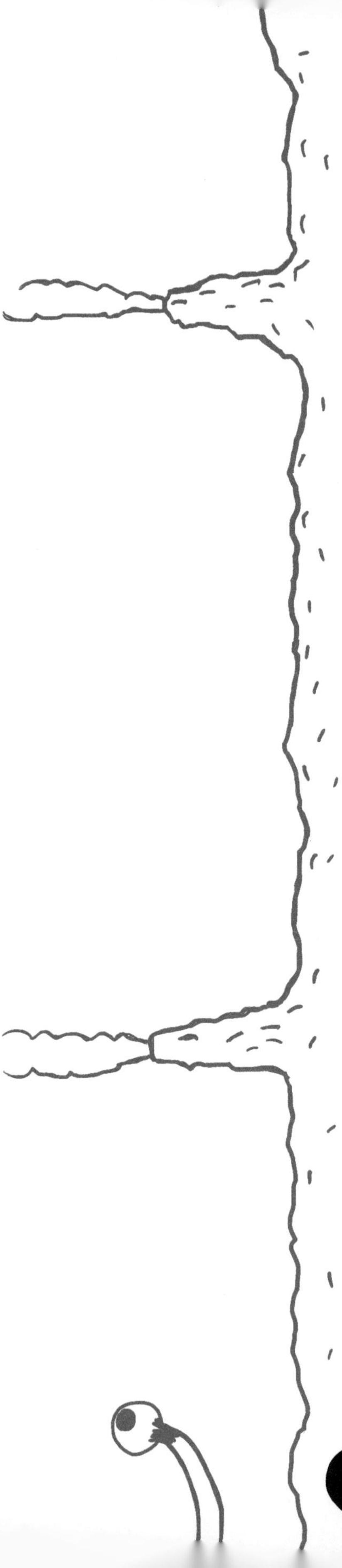

STICK SOME COINS ON THIS PAGE USING TAPE. CLOSE THE KOOB AND ASK A PARENT HOW MUCH THEY THINK THIS BOOK IS WORTH.

WHATEVER THEY SAY, OPEN THE KOOB
AND TURN TO THIS PAGE TO COUNT
UP THE COINS AND PROVE THEM WRONG!

If fireworks were black, does that mean the sky would have to be multicoloured?

Colour the sky around these fireworks with as many colours as you can.

Tie your tongue in a knot by saying these tongue-twisters as quickly as you can.

SHE SELLS SEASHELLS BY THE SEASHORE.

Red lorry, yellow lorry.

PETER PIPER PICKED A PECK OF PICKLED PEPPERS.

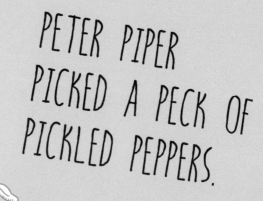

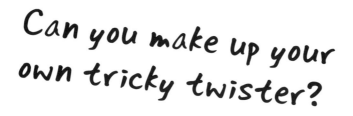

Can you make up your own tricky twister?

EVEN AN UPSIDE-DOWN WORLD CAN SEEM NORMAL AT TIMES!

ARE THESE STAIRS GOING UP OR DOWN?

Use these images to create a flickbook in your koob.

Cut out then stick all 64 squares over the even page numbers in the koob. The number on the back of each square tells you which page to stick it on.

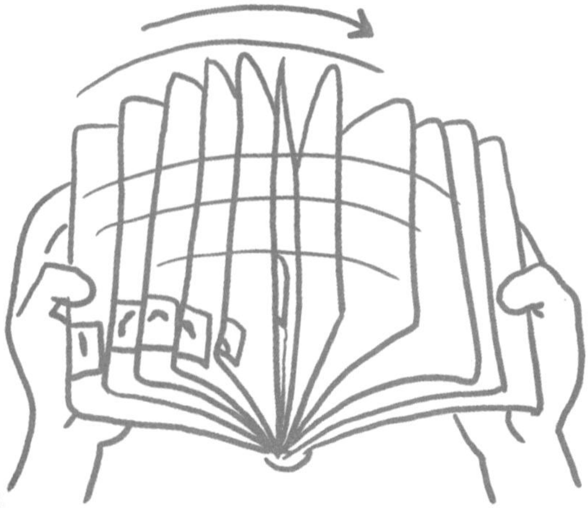

You can then flick the koob uʍop ǝpısdn or the right way up and watch the animation.

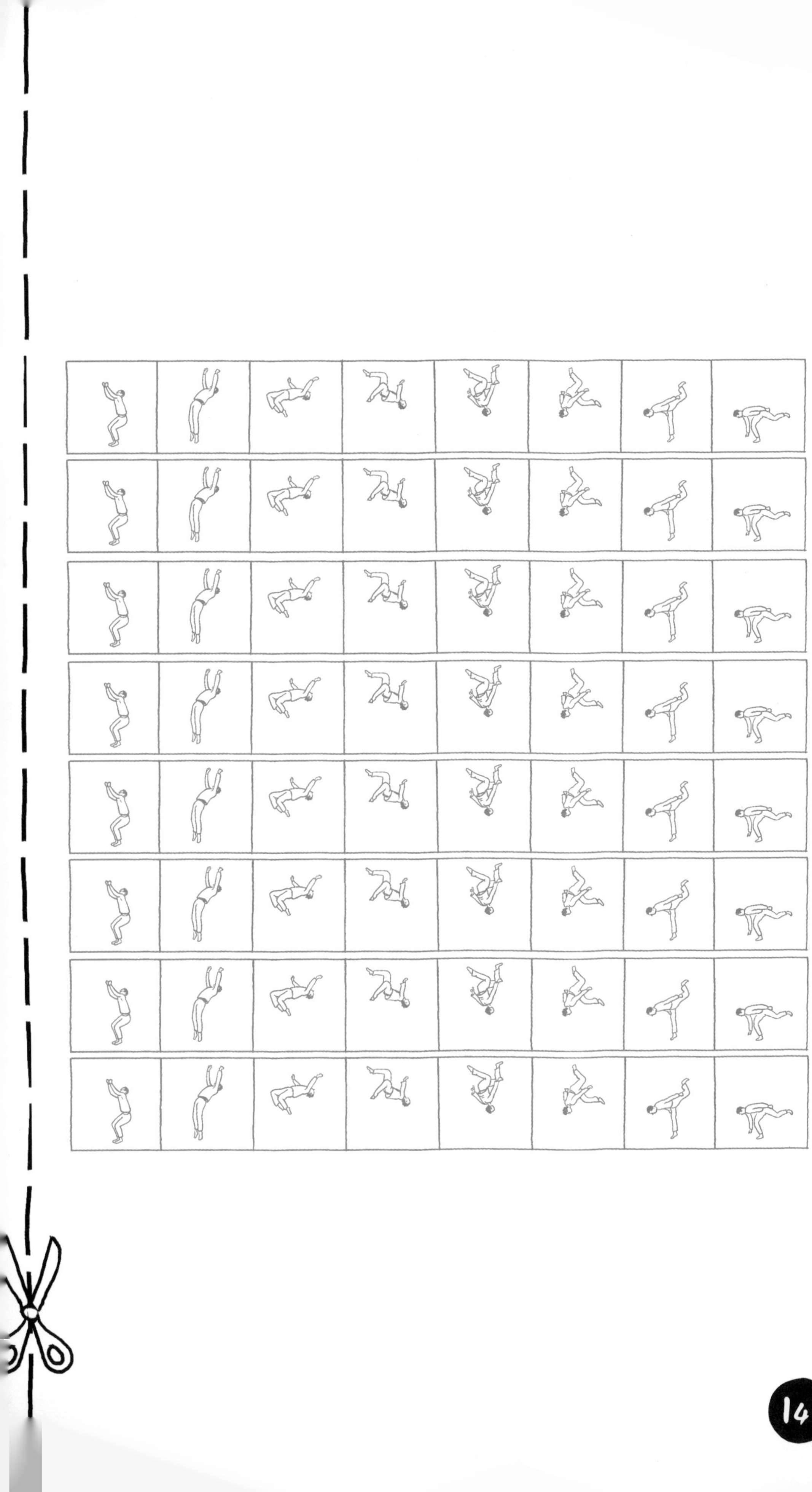

2	4	6	8	10	12	14	16
18	20	22	24	26	28	30	32
34	36	38	40	42	44	46	48
50	54	56	58	60	64	68	70
74	76	78	80	82	86	88	90
94	96	98	100	102	104	106	108
110	114	116	118	120	122	124	126
128	130	132	134	136	138	140	144